Business Credit Secrets

Save Your Company. How to Check and Repair a Negative Credit Score for Corporate Loans. Strategies To Solve Your Company's Liquidity Crisis Even Without Bank Money.

Author: Tony Risk

INTRODUCTION		**6**
CHAPTER 1.	**THE COMPANY RATING**	**8**
CHAPTER 2.	**HOW BANKS EVALUATE RELIABILITY**	**15**
CHAPTER 3.	**TYPES OF RATING**	**21**
CHAPTER 4.	**HOW IT IS CALCULATED**	**25**
720 AND ABOVE EXCELLENT		26
680-719-GOOD		26
620-679-AVERAGE		26
580-619-POOR		27
500-579-BAD		27
LESS THAN 500		27
CHAPTER 5.	**EVALUATION METHODS**	**29**
METHOD ONE: THE GUIDELINE PUBLIC COMPANY METHOD		29
METHOD TWO: THE GUIDELINE COMPANY TRANSACTION METHOD		31
RULES OF THUMB		34
CHAPTER 6.	**HOW TO CHECK YOUR CORPORATE CREDIT SCORE FOR FREE**	**36**
REASONS TO CHECK YOUR CREDIT REPORT		38
CHAPTER 7.	**THE BANK RATING**	**42**
CHAPTER 8.	**HOW TO TALK TO BANKS: ENTER THE HEADS OF BANKS**	**44**
GETTING ORGANIZED		44
BE PREPARED — BOY SCOUT MOTTO		44
DO YOU NEED A BUSINESS PLAN?		48
BORROWER BEWARE!		49
BUSINESS LOAN PROPOSAL		50
CHAPTER 9.	**HOW YOU CAN IMPROVE YOUR CREDIT SCORE**	**51**
CREDIT HABITS		52
CREATING A PLAN		54
WHAT YOU SHOULD RECORD		55
DON'T OVERTHINK IT		56
CHAPTER 10.	**THE 7 BUSINESS CRISIS INDICATORS**	**57**
CHAPTER 11.	**SAVE YOUR COMPANY**	**60**

STOP WITH THE NEW DEBT 60
RANK THE DEBT USING INTEREST RATES 60
SEE IF YOU CAN LOWER INTEREST RATES 61
CREATE YOUR OWN BUDGET 62
CREATE YOUR OWN REPAYMENT SCHEDULE 63
BE KIND TO YOURSELF 63

CHAPTER 12. LEARN TO BUILD A CORPORATE CREDIT 65

CHAPTER 13. FREE YOUR MIND TO FREE YOUR COMPANY FROM DEBT 73

THE GOOD DEBT 74
WHAT IS BAD DEBT? 75

CHAPTER 14. THE TYPICAL MISTAKES OF A GROWING COMPANY. 79

CHAPTER 15. STRATEGIES TO SOLVE YOUR COMPANY'S CRISIS 85

CHAPTER 16. COMPANY BUDGET: FINANCIAL INDICATORS, CASH FLOW. ... 91

WHEN YOUR FIRM USES ACCOUNTS RECEIVABLE – HOW TO PREDICT WHAT YOU'LL COLLECT WHEN 92
TRACK YOUR INFLOWS 94
WHEN POSSIBLE, USE DIRECT TRACING 94

CHAPTER 17. CREDIT RISK: HOW TO BEST MANAGE DELAYS AND INSOLVENCIES 97

AVOID LATE PAYMENTS 101
AUTO PAY 102
REMINDERS 102
WEEKLY PAYMENTS 102
CALL YOUR LENDER 103

CHAPTER 18. FINANCIAL PLANNING AND FINANCING REQUESTS: YOU DECIDE THE CONDITIONS OF YOUR FINANCING 104

ANALYSIS AND DIAGNOSIS 105
ESTABLISHING OBJECTIVES 106
IMPLEMENTING PLANS 107

CHAPTER 19. COMPANY C.V: HOW TO PRESENT THE COMPANY TO THE BANK. 108

BUSINESS CENTER MODEL 111

CHAPTER 20. REAL AND PERSONAL GUARANTEES 115

CHAPTER 21. HOW TO PROTECT YOUR CREDIT? 118

CHAPTER 22.   CORPORATE LOANS: THERE ARE NOT ONLY BANKS............ 123
- ONLINE LENDERS.. 123
- ANGEL INVESTORS 124
- VENTURE CAPITALISTS 124
- GRANTS... 125

CHAPTER 23.   CROWD FUNDING AND OTHER NON-BANK LOANS 126
- BORROW MONEY FROM FRIENDS AND FAMILY.................................. 126
- USE A CREDIT CARD... 127
- USE FUNDS FROM YOUR 401(K) 128
- CROWD FUND YOUR BUSINESS... 128
- GET AN SBA LOAN 129
- GET A MICROLOAN 131

CHAPTER 24.   ADVANTAGES OF A GOOD CREDIT SCORE 133
- BETTER CHANCE OF LOAN APPROVAL 133
- GET LOW INTEREST RATES ON LOANS... 134
- BETTER RATES ON CAR INSURANCE 134
- BETTER INTEREST RATES ON MORTGAGE 135
- BETTER CHANCE OF GETTING A JOB 136
- LOWER SECURITY DEPOSITS.. 136
- BETTER CHANCE OF APPROVAL FOR CREDIT CARDS 137
- HAVE MORE NEGOTIATING POWER 138

CHAPTER 25.   SIMPLE STRATEGIES TO FIX YOUR CREDIT 140

CHAPTER 26.   DEALING WITH UNFORESEEN CIRCUMSTANCES AND SUDDEN CATASTROPHES   144
- JOB LOSS 144
- INJURY AND ILLNESS... 147

CHAPTER 27.   PERSONAL OR BUSINESS CREDIT CARD?........................ 151
- THE DO'S AND DON'TS OF MANAGING YOUR CREDIT 151
- THE SECRET TO SUCCESS 153

CHAPTER 28.   PROTECTING YOUR FINANCIAL PRIVACY 155

CHAPTER 29.   YOUR FINANCIAL FREEDOM 159
- WHAT IS MEANT BY FINANCIAL FREEDOM?..................................... 159
- CREDIT CARDS AND FINANCIAL FREEDOM - IS IT SAFE? 160
- THE BEST HABITS TO HELP YOU REACH AND PROTECT YOUR FINANCIAL FREEDOM 161

CHAPTER 30.   HOW TO GET LENDER OFFERS? 166

CHAPTER 31. THE BEST WAYS TO MAXIMIZE YOUR CREDIT SCORE 168

    LINES OF CREDIT.. 173

CHAPTER 32. MANAGING FORECLOSURE/ BANKRUPTCY/TAX LIEN AND OTHER JUDGMENTS. 175

    WHAT IS FORECLOSURE? 175
    NOW, BANKRUPTCY? 176

CONCLUSION.. 179

Introduction

Credit is the single most influential factor in determining how we live today. On a personal level, your credit tells a story about you to potential employers, insurance companies, banks, and schools. Your credit also impacts the ability to obtain necessities like a home, a car and make personal lifestyle choices.

Though credit is fully entrenched in our society most people know very little about it. After you read this, you will understand fully how and why credit works the way it does. You will know what your credit score is, what it means, how to manage it, how to get a copy of your credit report, and use it to control your financial life successfully. With these tools you will become your own personal credit expert.

Basic Credit Terms

Let's begin with explaining some terms:

Credit Report. A credit report is a detailed history of your credit information. It begins the first day you open a financial account in your name such as a bank account, student loan, or credit card. At that point you have created a credit history which will now become part of your ongoing credit report. It generally includes current information on balances and payment history of your various debts. There is information on mortgages, car loans, home equity loans, student loans, and credit cards, plus any negative credit reporting such as delinquent payments and bankruptcies.

NOTE: The history of any credit card you close will remain on your credit report for seven years.

Also — and this may surprise you — essential personal data such as your social security number, date of birth, employment history, and alias are listed as well. So you can now see how important this report is, and how essential it is to keep an eye on it.

Credit Score. Anyone who has ever applied for a loan has heard about "checking their credit score" for eligibility. Generally it is a number based on everything in your credit report which instantly tells a potential creditor about you financially. One of the most popular scoring models used to calculate credit scores is called Fair Isaacs Corporation (FICO). Scores range from 300 to 850, and your score determines whether or not you will be considered for a car loan, a credit card, a mortgage, or any application you make for credit, and how much interest you will be charged. Like many things in life, the higher your score the better because it tells the lender the likelihood of being paid back for their loan. A score of 750 and above is generally considered top tier.

NOTE: Please remember scores go up and down. If your score is low (600 and below) that does not mean you are a bad person — it just means you need help managing your debt and credit. Fortunately, the Life & Debt system will do that for you.

Credit Bureaus. They keep own credit reports for you based on information provided to them by your credit card and loan companies. This includes payment history, how much and how often you make payments and your balance on each. You are entitled to a free copy of your report every year from all three credit bureaus and I recommend you get each one. Your credit score can vary from bureau to bureau due to the fact that not all of your financial information, which is supplied by creditors, is reported to each one.

Having good credit is essential to achieving financial and personal goals. There is nothing you can do, from applying for a new credit card or car loan, to making a late payment or filing for bankruptcy, that will not affect your credit score — and many things might surprise you.

Chapter 1. The Company Rating

When you carry out a company valuation or rating, you'll be looking at a number of factors.

- *You'll be looking at estimates of future returns - what cash flow the business is going to deliver. A really basic example - an investor buying shares in an income fund will assess the investment by looking at the yield, that is, how much he will get in dividends as a percentage of the price paid. 5% is better than 4.5% - all other things being equal.*
- *You'll be looking at comparisons with other businesses or assets. If a comparable business is rated at ten times earnings, that's a basis for assessing what yours might be worth. It might need to be adjusted up or down. Again, a really basic example is looking at houses in the same street - if one is worth $200,000, then a house with the same number of bedrooms and the same size garden further down the road is probably worth much the same, but you might need to adjust that figure if it's in a bad state of repair, or if it needs a makeover.*

People sometimes say that an asset is worth 'what the market will bear'. Let's examine that a bit more closely. If you put an asset up for auction, and ensure it's well advertised, then you'll find out exactly what the market will bear - it's possible that two bidders will compete against each other to take the auction way beyond what you thought you'd get. Equally, it's possible a lowballed will be the only one to make a bid.

But where do the bidders get their idea of what to pay for the asset? They have most probably seen a similar asset for sale elsewhere and noted the price. That's comparison - the second basis for a business valuation. Business purchasers may also have worked out what buying a new piece of equipment could save them, perhaps by cutting their fuel costs or making their manufacturing process quicker and less costly - that's looking at estimates of future returns. The bidder might not always have done the sums, but simply says, "Hey, next time I buy a vehicle for my fleet, I'll get a hybrid, because the price is 10% more but I reckon I'll save 20% on fuel". That's not awfully scientific, but it works.

'What the market will bear' may be based on a market of relatively inexpert purchasers, or of purchasers who are wised up on exactly what valuation they believe applies, but business assets - whether that's a company, or stocks and shares - always have their price set on the basis of an analysis of the prospects for the business, and the valuation of similar businesses, whether that's explicit or simply understood.

Absolute vs. relative rating

An absolute valuation model assesses the business by looking at its future earnings, dividend yield or cash flow, and assessing what they are worth in today's money. There's no comparison to other businesses - which can be useful if, as with some disruptive tech companies, there's not a valid comparison out there; the only variable in the equation is the cost of capital or discount rate that you use to calculate the valuation.

A relative valuation on the other hand compares the company you're looking at with other businesses, usually competitors or peers in the same sector - so you'd compare an IT consultant with other consultancies, a consumer goods manufacturer with other similar manufacturers.

Relative valuations can, however, be made broader. For instance, if you were buying a house to rent it out, you could compare other income-generating assets such as bonds, investment funds, or commercial property, to find out which investment would deliver the best return. Sometimes it can be useful, instead of looking at the business sector a company is in, to consider the kind of value it delivers - if it's a mature company which delivers regular dividends, it might be best compared with other companies which are similarly mature.

Factors that can affect ratings:

When you're looking at a business, the valuation will generally depend on various factors. For instance, it will be affected by

- *Earnings - present and forecast.*
- *The physical assets employed in the business - what are they worth?*
- *Revenues - sometimes you'll look at sales value, because the company isn't profitable, or has low profitability for some reason.*
- *Intangible assets such as proprietary technology, goodwill, or brands.*

Many valuations are forward-looking - they are based on expectations of future benefits to come from owning the business. Even if your forecasts are a bit back-of-envelope, making an effort to predict future revenues and cash flows is always worthwhile.

The forward-looking nature of valuations explains why stock markets sometimes move rapidly in response to a missed earnings number. The market isn't just reacting to the shortfall - it's also downgrading its expectations of future earnings. That's one reason why when Intel downgraded its earnings advice by 2-4% in 2000 the shares fell 30%.

Think about it this way. You expected to get $100 this year. You expected that return to grow by 10% a year, so you'd get $110, $121, $133, then $146. Now, this year's return is cut to $96. You're $4 down, right?

Well, if you're looking forwards, you'd expect future returns to be lower, too, as you're starting from a lower base. So just assuming you'll still get 10% growth, but starting from $96 rather than $100, you'd get future returns of $105, $116, $127 and $140 - so over the whole period, you'd be $24 worse off. That's a more significant fall in the value of the business than the 4% downgrade made it appear.

That's rather a simplistic example but it gives you an idea of how a downgrade of this year's earnings can affect future expectations. In the case of Intel, the effect was particularly savage, and you could argue that since this downgrade came right at the top of the tech boom, the shares were also overvalued. Investors had drastically overestimated the growth rate of companies like Intel and IBM. (Markets tend to work rather like a piece of elastic - you can stretch it and stretch it, forever such a long time, but eventually it will snap back violently.)

Sometimes, the value to different buyers can be different. This is often seen when a business that's quoted on the stock exchange is acquired by a competitor or by a corporate raider - the value of the shares can increase dramatically. Stock exchange investors are buying a financial asset, and they can't do anything to change its value; they only own a small percentage of the shares. A corporate buyer, on the other hand, who takes 100% ownership, will be able to change the business's strategy, can probably cut duplicate costs, and will gain synergies that make the acquisition more valuable.

'Marriage value' is a concept from the real estate sector that describes the extra value that comes from combining the freehold and leasehold interests in a given property. It's a nice phrase that describes how putting two businesses together can be worth more than the sum of the parts.

Quality of earnings

As well as considering the basic numbers, you'll also want to think about the quality of the business and its earnings. This includes factors such as

- *'Moats' - This is what Warren Buffett calls sources of business differentiation that can keep returns high. For instance, a company might have patent protection for some of its products, or it may have a brand image other companies can't compete with (think Coca-Cola). A company with a good 'moat' has a better quality of earnings (that is, its earnings should be more sustainable) than its competitors.*

- *Scalability - whether the business can grow without increasing its fixed costs. For instance, eBay is scalable, because it costs nothing to add another customer. Waban, on the other hand, wasn't scalable, because although it was an internet retailer, it did its own delivery - every 500 or so new customers, it had to buy another delivery van. eBay is a huge business now - and Waban went bust.*

- *Cyclicality. Some industries tend to work in cycles. That's the case with heavily capital-intensive sectors such as mining or chemicals; often (not always) it's driven by commodity prices. When things are going well, everyone invests in new plant. But the new plant isn't profitable at once, because it's only working at a small percentage of capacity, so earnings fall. And if all the businesses in the sector have new plant coming onstream at the same time, the effect is even worse. Earnings fall, and the business valuation falls - until, gradually, the plant fills up (sometimes because revenues grow, and sometimes because one or two competitors give up and leave the sector). Cyclical earnings are relatively low quality, and timing can be a big factor in making a successful purchase or sale.*

Make sure, if you're valuing a business in an industry you don't know well, to take a look at the general background trends.

- *Is the industry growing or shrinking? Is it consolidating? Acquiring smaller businesses in an industry that's consolidating can be a way to gain greater purchasing power and clean up - but it can also be relatively high risk.*
- *Are there any disruptive technologies that compete with the business you're looking at? They can quickly kill the preceding generation. In 1984, Kodak was by far the leader in the US photographic market. In the 1990s, though, it was slow to launch a digital camera; it got the market wrong, seeing digital cameras as expensive luxuries rather than commodities, and so its cameras were over-specified and made at too high a cost. By 2012, it had to file for bankruptcy. Right now, the automotive industry looks at risk - electric cars, self-driving cars, and hybrids represent a huge investment on which car firms are mostly making very little money.*
- *Is the basis of sales changing? From 2000 onwards many software companies moved from selling one-time software licenses to selling subscriptions (Software as a Service, or SaaS). For many of them, that's been a really good deal - but they suffered several years of earnings disruption as instead of selling $50,000 a license, they were only making $15,000 or so a year in subscriptions on the same client.*
- *Is regulation tightening up? When government starts taking notice of what has generally been an unregulated industry,*

that can increase costs and even put some firms out of business.

Going concern vs liquidation value
A business that is operating, and making profits, or is likely to make them in future, sells on the basis of those profits. It's a going concern and it's valued in the expectation that it will continue in business and carry on making profits.

On the other hand, sometimes a business is staring extinction in the face. A company that still has only analogue products that are being replaced by digital services isn't going to last long. That doesn't mean it's worth nothing. But you wouldn't value it on the going concern basis. Instead, you'd look at what the different assets are worth if it's broken up and everything is sold off. That's its liquidation value.

Chapter 2. How Banks Evaluate Reliability

The bank makes loans available to people with the expectation that the money will be paid back to it within the mutually agreed time. It is reasonable to believe that people borrow money from the bank with the expectation and intention to repay the loans when they are due. However, things do not always go as planned or intended. It has been observed that some people who obtain loans from the bank, especially entrepreneurs, are unable to repay the loans when they ought to do so. Such people usually start telling cock and bull stories when it is time to repay their loans.

It is not the expectation of the bank that the beneficiaries of its loan facilities will be unable to repay the loans they collect from it for any reason, when the lifespan of the loans expire. Such breach of contract has serious legal consequences. In addition, it also has the tendency of destroying (rather than cementing) the relationships between the bank and the beneficiaries of its loan facilities. Being aware of these, money-lending processes and procedures are designed to checkmate this occurrence.

It is worthy of note that, sometimes, bank officials who relate with the bank's clients on behalf of the bank, not the bank itself, shoulder the burden of responsibilities of inabilities of borrowers to repay the loans they obtain from the bank. Consequently, the bank has some laid down processes, procedures, structures, terms and conditions for lending money to people which ensure that only suitably qualified loan applicants, otherwise called eligible borrowers, are the exclusive beneficiaries of its loan.

There are basic requirements for obtaining bank loan as an entrepreneur. They are the conditions people must satisfy before getting business loan. They are as follows:

1. Evidence of ability to repay the loan

This is the first and most important factor that entices the bank when entrepreneurs approach it for loans. The bank wants to be convinced beyond every reasonable doubt that the beneficiaries of its loan facilities will be able to repay the loans, even with ease, when they ought to do so. The bank wants to be reasonably certain that the beneficiaries of its loan facilities will have neither delay nor challenge repaying the loans that are made available to them.

The bank usually ascertains this from the track record of high profitability and high cash flow of the business the prospective borrower intends to finance with the loan. It is instructive to note that the most reliable document the bank usually uses to ascertain the profitability and cash flow of a business is its financial statements. This is why the bank hardly gives loan to start-up businesses. It is obvious that a start-up business cannot have a financial statement.

For as long as a prospective borrower who applies for business loan is able to convince the bank beyond every reasonable doubts that he has the ability, capacity and financial strength to pay back the loan within the stipulated time; it is very unlikely that he will be denied of the loan by the bank. In a situation this cannot be reasonably ascertained, the prospective borrower should be certain that he will be denied of his request, even without any regret or delay.

2. Corporate Financial Statements

It was remarked that the most reliable document the bank usually uses to ascertain the profitability and cash flow of a business is its financial statements. The corporate financial statements, i.e. the financial statements of a company's bank account, are usually the most reliable evidence for ascertaining the ability of a prospective borrower to repay a loan. The statement of account must be for the business the prospective borrower intends to fund with the loan.

There are some implications of this. The first implication is that any entrepreneur who wants to obtain bank loan should approach the bank as a corporate entity, not as an individual. The second implication is that the entrepreneur should have a corporate bank account. He should present his corporate financial statement(s) to the bank through the bank(s) his organization has (an) account(s) with, if the organization has no account with the bank.

The bank is very interested in the statement of account of a business because it helps to ascertain the cash flow and financial strength of a business. The loan the bank will (be willing to) offer a prospective borrower will always be determined by the cash flow of his business. In other words, the commercial loan the bank offers a borrower is usually within the range of the amount of money the organization controls, as shown in the corporate financial statements.

The bank considers it a suicide mission when a would-be borrower applies for an amount of money that is far higher than his business controls. This is why such requests are easily turned down without any second thought. Perhaps, this is in fidelity to the biblical claim that whoever cannot be trusted in a little thing cannot be trusted in a big thing. It is the expectation of the bank that the growth of a business will be gradual and progressive, not sudden.

The bank is also interested in Bank Account Integrity when it requests the financial statement of a business from a prospective borrower. There are two major factors that determine the integrity of a bank account or financial statement. The first factor is the amount of money that passes through the bank account. As earlier remarked, the loan the bank will (be willing to) offer a prospective borrower will always be determined by the cash flow of his business.

3. The Purpose of a Loan

Bank loans are usually requested to fund predetermined purposes. Business loans, in the recommendation of the bank, should be exclusively used to fund specific commercial, entrepreneurial or business projects. The bank demands information on the purpose of a business loan as part of the requirements for considering whether to grant it or not. Borrowers are not expected to determine what to do with a bank loan after applying for the loan.

The bank always demands a clear, precise and unambiguous description of the purpose a business loan is intended for in order to ascertain that it is feasible, practicable, viable and reasonable. The bank will reject an application for a business loan from a prospective borrower if this condition is not satisfied. In addition, the bank will also reject an application for a business loan (with ease) if the purpose of the loan is not compatible with its policy.

There are some purposes the bank will not identify with when it is approached for a business loan. For example, the bank will ever give loan for the funding of any business that is prohibited by the law. The bank will ever associate itself with funding any illegal objective. In addition, it is very unlikely that the bank will give loan to an entrepreneur to fund a project that is not income-generating in nature e.g. payment of school fees, house rent, medical bill, etc.

4. Projection Data

Prior to applying for a business loan, in addition to being clear about the purpose the loan will be used to fund, a prospective borrower is expected to have projections of what he hopes to achieve with the loan, and also how he hopes to achieve that. The bank is very interested in the data that are used in making the projections. The bank is very interested in the approximate potential profits of a business an entrepreneur intends to fund with a business loan.

The projection data assist the bank to ascertain that the prospective objective, project or business of a probable, would-be or potential borrower is feasible, reasonable, realistic, practicable, profitable and viable. The data for the projections must also be credible and reasonable. In addition, the data must suggest that the business has higher probability of success than failure before the bank will make the loan for its funding available to the borrower.

5. Cash Cycle

An organization may not be paid by the client(s) immediately it executes a business activity. It may wait for days, weeks or months before it receives payments for the products it supplies to the clients, or for the services it renders to them. The time between the performance or execution of a business activity and the payment for the business activity is called Cash Cycle. The bank is very interested in the information to enable it to predict (almost) accurately when a borrower will be able to pay back a loan.

6. . Relationship

The bank usually prefers giving loans to individuals or organizations that are already known to it. Such people or organizations are those that already have a relationship with it. It is the expectation of the bank that giving loan to an individual or an organization will strengthen its relationship with the customer. The best relationship an individual or an organization will have with the bank is being its customer. This involves having an active account with the bank.

But why does the bank prefer people or organizations that have relationship with it to be the beneficiaries of its loans? The reason is that loans are usually attached to the customers' bank accounts. The process is usually structured in such that borrowers receive payments from their client(s) through their accounts with the bank. With such arrangement, the bank easily deducts its money from the borrower's account with it when the client(s) make(s) payment(s).

7. Collateral

Collateral was defined as a valuable a borrower offers a lender before receiving a loan from him/it. Collateral is a necessary precondition for getting a bank loan because it ensures the bank from losing its money. It is instructive to note that since the bank does not expect that the beneficiaries of its loans will not be able to repay the loans when they ought to do so; their primary interest in ascertaining the eligibility of probable borrowers is not collateral.

This is why the bank may still deny a loan applicant the financial assistance he requests, even when he has good collateral. Though collateral is usually a requisite for collecting a bank loan, it becomes important only when all the other factors and conditions are satisfied. Consequently, the ability to provide collateral is inadequate to certify that someone or an organization is an eligible borrower. It is necessary but insufficient for getting bank loan.

The most important requirement for getting bank loan is the ability of the prospective borrower to repay the loan. This is the single or overall factor the bank is most interested in. If you take a close look at all the requirements for getting bank loan above, you would observe that their purposes revolve around ascertaining the repayment ability of a would-be borrower. The bank will grant a loan for as long as it can ascertain the repayment ability of the borrower.

The above are the basic and fundamental requirements for getting a commercial (or business) loan from the bank to fund a business. Each of the requirements plays a vital role in ensuring the success of the contractual and business relationship.

Chapter 3. Types of Rating

Present Value of Cash Flow

Lenders are constantly working with borrowers to try to restructure cash flow. At its essence this is the very nature of a loan—the borrower gets initial positive cash flow (the loan is advanced), followed by a long period of relatively small negative cash flow (the loan is serviced with interest and periodic principal payments), followed by a final large negative cash flow (the balloon payment at maturity, assuming that is the loan structure). Lenders are also working with borrowers to negotiate upfront fees, closing costs and prepayment provisions. The variance of the timing of negative and positive cash flow to the borrower requires that lenders understand the present value of cash flow.

Present value of cash flow, also called discounted value, is the current worth of future money discounted at a specified interest rate. The higher the discount rate, the lower the present value of future cash flows. The theory behind present value of cash flow is simple but lenders need to be aware of how to use discount values to mitigate risk, maximize loan value and correctly market their services to lenders.

To this end, it is imperative that a lender calculates the present value of each basis point of the loan for its expected life. Calculators are readily available, and the authors have a number of these excel spread sheets to share. For example, if a lender knows that one basis point of loan spread is worth $1,000, then a lender can increase the profitability of the loan by offsetting an upfront fee with an increase in spread as long as the sum profit for the bank is maximized.

We have seen smart lenders win borrowers over by waiving upfront fees but embedding much larger profitability into the loan spread, or vice versa, depending on the borrower's goals and sensitivities. Conversely, we have witnessed lenders surprised to lose borrowers at the closing table and forgo substantial loan fees—however, a simple present value calculation would demonstrate that the loan fee the borrower is forgoing is a pittance relative to the present value of the cash flow the borrower is saving by taking a competing lower spread loan.

Forward Rates

While the yield curve shows interest rates from today to a point in the future, the forward curve is defined as the future expectation of a specific interest rate index. For example, we know exactly where Prime is today, and it is possible to discern where the market expects Prime to be tomorrow, the next day and so on. This forward or implied rate for Prime is shown in the graph below. We can also construct a forward curve for another index, such as Treasuries, LIBOR or Fed Funds. The forward index can be for short-term rates (Prime, 1-month LIBOR, Fed Funds) or for long-term rates (5 or 10-year Treasuries or swap rates).

The forward curve is very important for lenders to understand because it too motivates borrowers' behavior—just as the term structure of interest rates does. Again, borrowers are motivated by fear and greed. In an upwardly sloping forward interest rate environment, where interest rates are expected to be higher in the future than they are today, a borrower's natural fear motivates locking in longer fixed rates; however, the countervailing greed instinct motivates a borrower to take a chance with lower rates today in the hope that the forward curve is wrong.

Conversely, in a downward sloping forward interest rate environment, where interest rates are expected to be lower in the future than they are today, a borrower's natural greed and fear are aligned and motivates the borrower to lock in the forward rates because the borrower eliminates the uncertainty or rate movement and obtains a lower rate by locking in a longer-term fixed rate.

A lender's knowledge of the forward curve also helps mitigate the bank's risk of lending in a specific expected interest rate environment. Each lender must consider the impact of possible higher rates on the borrower's ability to service the loan. If rates are lower in the future as the loan reprocess on a shorter index, the borrower's debt-service coverage improves. However, if rates in the future are higher as the loan reprocess on a shorter index, the borrower's debt-service coverage diminishes unless cash flow (EBITDA or NOI) can increase. In a rising rate environment, it is critical for lenders to be able to assess the borrower's ability to service debt, as even small deviation from the base case can force strong initial credits to become susceptible to cash flow impairment. Regulators typically want to see interest rate stress tested at 3.00% from the implied forward rate and at that level, many borrowers at initial DSC ratios of 1.4X cannot service the debt.

Floors

Lenders impose interest rate floors on floating rate loans to augment yield and prevent loan yields from falling below an acceptable level. The value of the floor is determined by four factors: 1) floor level, 2) volatility of interest rates, 3) loan amount and 4) time term of the floor. A floor is more valuable to a lender if the floor level is higher, volatility of interest rates is higher, the amount of the loan is larger, and the term of the floor is longer.

Lenders should be aware of two main issues around floors: 1) floors have maximum value if the floor level is below the starting loan rate, and 2) the value of the floor is minimal if the borrower has an option to prepay the loan.

By setting a floor level below the starting floating loan rate, the lender protects margin in the event that interest rates fall. However, when interest rates are low and lenders are attempting to extract higher yield to make up for a retail funding disadvantage by instituting floors above the starting index plus loan spread, certain negative consequences arise. For example, assume that a loan is priced at Prime flat, but the floor is set above the starting Prime rate—this is called an "in-the-money" floor. Borrowers may believe that they are a prime-based customer; nonetheless, many borrowers are willing to live with an in-the-money floor—which in their opinion is a temporary cost.

The issue is that when interest rates increase, the lender's cost of funding will rise but the loan yield will not increase until the floor is reached; therefore, the lenders' NIM will compress. Furthermore, the floor may cause negative convexity, which is a fancy way of saying that when rates rise, and the floor is bumped, borrowers will prepay the loan. This is the second issue with floors—if there is no prepayment protection on the loan, borrowers will prepay the loan at their option, which usually is at the disadvantage of the lender.

Caps and Collars

An interest rate cap works the same way as a floor except that it protects the holder of the cap from interest rates rising. The same principles apply to a cap as to a floor. The value of the cap is determined by the following factors: 1) cap level, 2) volatility of interest rates, 3) loan amount and 4) time term of the cap. A cap is more valuable to a lender if the cap level is lower, volatility of interest rates is higher, the amount of the loan is higher, and term of the floor is longer.

Chapter 4. How It Is Calculated

How is your credit score calculated? While it varies a little between the different credit reporting companies, the basic rules are the same. Some of the major factors that go into the algorithm to determine your score include things like debt level, credit history, and payment behavior. There is no consistent way in which they are measured since the weight of each is dependent on all the other credit factors available. Factors like ethnicity, religion and gender are not taken into consideration.

Your FICO score is a measure of the overall quality of your credit. While it is not the only available metric for determining credit score, it is the one that is most commonly used by a wide range of different lenders and companies when it comes to determining the level of risk that is associated with a given individual.

It is based on a handful of different categories at various levels of importance to the total. It has been determined that payment history is weighted with approximately 35 percent relevance, the amount owed has a 30 percent relevance, credit history length has a 15 percent relevance, abundance of new credit has a 10 percent relevance and the type of credit used has a 10 percent relevance.

It also factors in things such as delinquency, number of accounts you have in collections, bankruptcy and how long it has been since these problems appeared on your record. As such, the greater number of problems you have had in this regard, the worse your overall FICO score is going to be.

When it comes to the amount you currently owe to lenders, FICO takes into account the amount of debt you currently have as well as the types of accounts you hold and the number of different accounts that you currently hold.

To help you understand the scores better, here is a breakdown of the credit score ranges and what each means.

720 and Above Excellent

When you have this score, you get the best interest rates and repayment terms for all loans. This score can come in handy if you are hoping to make some major purchases. You will be able to get credit without any problems and at the lowest possible rates. But then, this score is extremely hard to establish. You will have to put in a lot of effort to maintain this score and still, you will not come anywhere close to 800. The most you can wish to come close to is 720 and remain there for as long as possible.

680-719-Good

When you are in this category, you will get good rates and terms but not as good as those with excellent scores. With this score, you can get favorable mortgage terms. You might not face as many problems but will have to be ready to run around from company to company to have your credit approved. Again, this score is not very common. You need to put in extra effort to get it over the 680 mark. If because of some erroneous charges you are not able to cross this limit, then you must try your best to get it cleared as soon as possible.

620-679-Average

When you are in this category, you can get fair mortgage terms and have it easy when buying smaller ticket items, (of course with no better rate than good and excellent scores). Take care not to slip down to the level where mortgage is unaffordable.

580-619-Poor

When you are at this level, you only get credit on the lenders' terms. You will probably pay more to access credit so be ready to pay more. Also, you should remember that you cannot access auto financing if your score goes lower than this range so you should work towards building it. This is where a large majority lie. Their score will be bad mostly owing to wrong entries. If you lie here, then you will have a tough time getting credit in your budget limits and will have to be ready to pay up a lot of money.

500-579-Bad

If your credit score is in this range, access to credit will cost you dearly. Actually, if you are looking for a 30-year mortgage, you could be looking at, at least 3% higher interest rates than how much you would pay if you had good credit. On the other hand, if you are looking for something short time like a 36-month auto loan, you will probably pay almost double the interest rate you would pay if you had good credit. So being here is probably the worst thing that can happen to your credit report. You cannot possibly be here and hope to get away with low interest rates.

Less than 500

If your credit score goes to this level, it is so bad that it might be almost impossible to get any type of financing. If you do, the interest rate will simply be unfathomable. You might have to spend 30 to 40 years trying to repay it. Your entire life will be dedicated toward repaying a loan and you might only get free by the time you are 50.

I am sure several of you are in this last range. But do not panic as help is at hand. You might wonder if it is possible for you to fix your score if you are in this category and the answer is yes! It is possible for you to improve your credit score and possibly enter the good range.

Chapter 5. Evaluation Methods

Method One: The Guideline Public Company Method

The guideline public company method (GPCM) is widely used to value medium to large closely held companies when the appraiser can locate publicly traded comparable companies (called "comps"). Smaller businesses can also be appraised using this approach given the substantive number of micro-capitalization stocks traded on the NASDAQ exchange. Pink sheet stocks (unregulated markets), or the exchange they transact on, is not considered to be an "active market." The appraiser should avoid using pink sheet stocks as comparable companies under this method.

When It's Used

Valuations for tax-related purposes must at least consider the market approach. Fair market value is the standard used for tax-related appraisals. As the adoption of the fair market value standard has flourished and Revenue Ruling 59-60's prescription has increased as a guiding light for other appraisal purposes; today the market approach is widely considered and applied in many business valuations that extend beyond tax-related engagements.

When considered a candidate for the market approach, the appraiser will search for publicly traded companies that are similar to the subject closely held entity. Many "mom and pop" enterprises quickly disqualify from using this method due to the inadequacy of similar publicly traded companies. In addition to matching companies within a similar industry, size discrepancies can render a guideline company impractical. For example, using Google as a comparable company under the GPCM to estimate the value of a small online advertising company would be impractical due to the relative size discrepancy. Another problem is aligning revenue streams. Closely held companies are not only concentrated in sources of revenue, but also in customers. Having two or three customers representing half of an entity's total sales base is not unusual. On the flipside, many publicly traded companies diversify their revenue streams in both lines of business and customers. United Technologies (UTX) earns revenue from industries ranging from aerospace and defense to commercial refrigeration. Despite having one of the largest commercial refrigeration operations in the world, sales from the division are only a part of total revenue, which collectively includes defense, aerospace, elevators, HVAC, etc. Using UTX as a comparable company without division of segment lines in the valuation of a closely held commercial refrigeration company would be difficult to justify as appropriate. These are a few reasons why the guideline public company method is not always deemed proper.

The appraiser must also consider factors other than the industry when using the market approach. Tax courts have affirmed value conclusions using the market approach when the business appraiser used companies with similar economic characteristics that operated in differing industries. Companies with similar customer targets, seasonality, brand awareness and the like could be (and have been) used as successful comparable companies. The key determinant is that the comparable companies selected using the GPCM make economic sense.

Method Two: The Guideline Company Transaction Method

The guideline company transaction method (GCTM) is the other commonly used method under the market approach. Instead of relying on publicly traded company multiples to determine value, the GCTM uses multiples derived from actual transactions that have occurred. The appraiser then applies those multiples to the subject closely held company. Estimating a closely held company's value using merger and acquisition multiples (otherwise known as transaction multiples), this method is also known as the Merger and Acquisition Method.

When It's Used

Valuations for tax-related purposes must at least consider the market approach. The same standards and considerations noted in the guideline public company method apply. One of the principal impediments of using the guideline public company method is securing an adequate number of comparable publicly traded companies. Revenue Ruling 59-60 requires consideration of the market approach. Here's where the GCTM becomes especially advantageous.

Closely held companies, notably smaller firms, are typically single product or service focused businesses. Despite the company's industry, these businesses are usually fragmented. Many falls in the small to medium-size value range. Think of the local dentist, insurance agency, auto-repair center – any product or service offering that requires a local presence. Economies of scale afforded to multinational conglomerates are not possible for these types of firms. I'm not claiming that economies of scale aren't realizable at a smaller level – they are – but the level of scale is much lower on a comparable dollar level. Economies of scale are cost savings (advantages) received from increased size, whether size is defined as output or scale of operations.

Unlike the guideline public company method where information is abundant and free to access, closely held company transaction information can be difficult and costly to obtain. Closely held business owners of private businesses are not usually ecstatic about opening up their company's financial statements to third parties (and rightfully so). Some, however, agree to disclose information to service providers, especially if the transaction took place through a business broker. The extent of information provided by the business brokers often depends on the transacting parties' willingness to disclose information. Sometimes the entire "deal" (so to speak) is provided, whereas other times only particular multiples are given without full disclosure of owner compensation or other financial details. Hence, a degree of reporting bias is introduced into the data.

By subscribing to one of the available databases, appraisers can search for transactions applicable to the subject closely held company. Industry, geography and financial relativity (sales, for example) are used to narrow down deal multiples that best "fit" the subject entity.

The benefit of using transaction multiples is that they are frequently more relatable to the closely held company. Appraising the local dentist's office is nearly impossible to do using the guideline public company method. Dentistry is a fragmented industry, meaning dental offices are spread throughout the country, in both ownership and geography. Most dental practices consist of three or fewer practitioners per building, with many having just one. Database transaction information provides a more comparable level of value. Moreover, the transactions reported are real deals. They provide a direct indication of value.

Finally, the guideline company transaction method can be used as a test of reasonableness. Using dentistry as an example, we know that the guideline public company method is highly unlikely to be used under the market approach. Assume the closely held business being appraised is a specialty dentistry practice and few, if any, transactions are available for this particular niche. The income approach is deemed appropriate, but the market approach has been determined as not being reliable enough to provide a sound value estimate. Using the income approach to value the entity directly, the appraiser can "check" to see if the value estimate is reasonable using private transaction market multiples. In this case, the appraiser would find transactions similar to the specialty – perhaps general dentistry if the economic demand factors were congruent – and use those multiples as a test of reasonableness on the value conclusion derived from the income approach.

The force propelling the GCTM as a test of reasonableness lies in the understanding that while the transaction data failed to be reliable enough to calculate the closely held entity's value directly, the data is good enough to help ensure the value estimate isn't illogical. Business appraisals should read like a thesis paper with all appropriate support included. In many circumstances, the GCTM can aid the appraiser in supporting the argument, or conclusion of value.

Rules of Thumb

Rules of thumb populate every industry. Closely held business owners like to have a sense of what their company is worth. In many cases, rules of thumb provide a semi-accurate value estimate. Throughout my career, I've witnessed some industries to have (surprisingly) relatively accurate rule of thumb valuation estimates. What I've also gleaned is that annual sales figures tend to be the most reliable rule of thumb value indicator. An example would be to use two times sales (multiply two by last year's sales) to calculate the rule of thumb value estimate (again, this is very much driven by industry). EBITDA, on the other hand, is what most business owners like to suggest when discussing value. EBITDA serves a purpose in some industries when using a rule of thumb approach. Those industries are those that:

1) *Have the same capital structure (same debt to equity mix),*
2) *Have the same working capital requirements,*
3) *Have the same tax rate, legal structure, and depreciate fixed assets the same,*
4) *Spend the same amount on capital expenditures (Capex), and*
5) *Operate in an industry with zero real growth (the multiple never changes).*

Companies within a handful of industries have comparable attributes. For these industries, EBITDA can be applied as a rule of thumb to provide a semblance of value. EBITDA, however, is one of the crudest proxy cash flow multiples. It serves a purpose, especially in financial analysis, but EBITDA's use in the valuation of closely held companies can be cancerous.

When Rules of Thumb Are Used?

Here we're talking about using rules of thumb in valuations of closely held businesses. Rules of thumb fall under the market approach because each industry tends to have them. First, rules of thumb should not be used as a direct method to estimate a company's value. Unless each company in an industry is exactly the same and sells for the same pricing multiples, rules of thumb are useless for direct application in valuing companies.

However, (yes, there's a catch) rules of thumb can be useful when performing a test of reasonableness, which is a "sanity check" on the value conclusion. If a rule of thumb is used to perform a sanity check, the appraiser must perform enough research to assure that a statistical relationship exists between the rule of thumb and the value conclusion.

Chapter 6. How to Check Your Corporate Credit Score for Free

Checking the credit score for your business is just as important as checking your personal score. The reasons for checking the score are very similar. The one difference is that some companies offer credit cards to their employees. You should carefully check your reports for any issues which may come up with employee credit cards.

There are several places to check your business credit score. Dun & Bradstreet offer free checks via Credit Signal. The website will let you know if there are any significant changes, which can also be tracked through a mobile application or the online dashboard. The service is limited though – you can get more advanced checks but only if you sign up for a subscription at an extra cost.

Another option is Nav, which uses information from both Dun & Bradstreet and Experian. Nav will give your credit score and summarized credit reports. You will need to pay for a full credit report if that is what you want to see. An extra feature provided by Nav is the ability to set goals to help you increase your score.

Free reports can also be received from Sorely, which shows you how to improve your score easily. The company provides the data and some tips if your business credit is getting out of hand. You can get a paid subscription if you feel you need even more help and resources.

There are only a few places that give a free business credit score; most companies require a fee to provide this information. Some websites will let you check your business credit report for free, but it is only on a trial basis and you will not have access after a specified time period. You will usually get 7 or 30 working days for free and must then start to pay for the service.

Many businesses choose to pay for comprehensive credit reports as it is the only way to be certain of the facts. The three credit bureaus will charge you for your credit reports. Duns & Bradstreet use a D-U-N-S number and this service will require a payment of $159 per month but comes with many benefits. A credit report from Equifax costs $99.95 once-off. Experian offers a single Credit Score Report at $39.95, or a full credit report for $49.95.

A credit score gives an indication of how you handle your credit, but your credit record (or report) provides detailed information about your past and current credit situation. A credit report consists of four sections: identifying information, credit history, public filings, and inquiries. Checking your credit report is the first step to a better credit future and improved credit rating.

There are lots of reasons to check your credit score frequently. Some people check their credit records when a credit application is rejected unexpectedly. You do not want to fall victim to identity fraud and have money stolen – these types of transactions can be identified by inspecting your credit record. It is always good idea to carefully check your credit score before applying for loans. Another reason to check your credit record is to ensure any cosigned loans are being paid by the correct person. Checking your credit score and record allows you to identify any mistakes or issues before lasting damage is done.

Everyone is entitled to one free credit per year from the three main credit bureaus. There are several websites you can visit to request a credit report. Another option is to ask for your report to be sent via physical mail, but this action may incur a fee. Many of the websites are run by third parties who provide credit services. These companies offer a credit score update on a monthly basis so you can keep track of your credit actions. Businesses should have a good idea of their credit record since it is mostly based on making timely payments. However, it's a good idea to review your business's credit record. You can request a credit record from several places but there are not as many options as with personal credit scores. Additionally, your business will usually need to pay to receive a business credit report. Many companies offer credit management services to businesses and will provide you with a monthly credit report and advice but charge a fee for these services. Checking your personal and business credit score is a vital part of managing your finances. It is the first step to determining where you can improve your credit score. The credit record will help you in identifying any errors, and ultimately guide you in credit management decisions.

Reasons to Check Your Credit Report

Checking your credit score will quickly give you an idea of how you rate on FICO or Vantage Score. It will let you know whether you need to improve your score. The more important thing to investigate is the credit report. Your credit report will show all the transactions that affect your credit score. Looking at the report will help you to identify the areas in which you can improve your credit score. Here are some reasons to carefully review your credit record.

1. Rejected Credit Application

One of the major reasons to check your report is at times when someone denies your credit request. If you think that your credit score is good, then it may come as a shock if you are not approved for a credit card or home loan. There is always a reason behind the rejection, and you need to find out what the reason is as it could affect future applications.

Request a report from one of the three credit bureaus to see the reason. In most cases, a response on your credit application will be given in writing and mention which bureau was used for the check. You are then given 60 days from notification to pull a free credit report. The reason for the rejected application will be visible in the report. It might be that you currently have too much debt, or sometimes applications are turned down simply because a person does not have a good variety of credit.

Carefully check the report for any mistakes or questionable entries. For example, you may have paid an account in cash, but the creditor did not record the transaction, which makes it seem as if you have missed a payment. You need to take this up with the creditor and have the error corrected to fix your credit score. Another issue is identity theft where someone uses your identity to get access to credit. You may not know about this situation until your credit application is rejected.

2. Identity Fraud and Theft

The concepts of identity theft and identity fraud are very close. Identity theft happens when a perpetrator steals a person's personal information. This information may include your bank account details, social security number, and passwords. Identity fraud occurs when the stolen information is used in various ways. In other words, the perpetrator is pretending to be you and using your accounts for various transactions.

Some people quickly pick up that they are victims of identity fraud. For example, if you check your bank statement frequently and you see a transaction that you know you did not make, then someone else may have access to your account. You can visit the bank to sort out the situation and may even receive some of your money back. But what happens when a criminal uses your information to take out a new loan or apply for a credit card? You may not know that this is happening and only realize the problem if your credit application is later denied.

Checking your credit report frequently will help you to identify transactions like credit card applications, which you know you did not make. You will then need to take it up with the authorities and relevant credit bureaus to get rectify the situation. If you don't, you are at high risk. The perpetrator can continue to use your information and can ruin your credit score. Oftentimes, the only way to know if your identity has been stolen is by pulling a credit report.

3. Preparing for a Loan Application

A good time to check your credit record is before applying for a new loan. It is best to check the score several weeks before you intend to apply for a car financing or a home loan. An early check will reveal what you can improve on your credit report and you can then get to work ironing out those issues. Small outstanding amounts or mistakes on your credit record can have a big impact on your credit score. Settle any outstanding amounts, especially if they are late or if the amounts are very small. Any mistakes on your credit report should be rectified before proceeding with an application. If you know you want to buy a house next year, then now is a great time to check your credit score as you will have at least a year to improve it before applying for loans.

4. Surety and Cosigning Concerns

Sometimes a person needs a little help with their finances, and you jump in to help. Your daughter may want to purchase her first car but since she just graduated and doesn't have a solid credit record, the bank is hesitant to finance the vehicle for her. The bank may be willing to provide a vehicle loan, but she needs someone to cosign the loan. You agree to sign the contract with her, but this means you are now also bound by the debt and your daughter's actions.

In this situation you have cosigned the loan; some lenders call this a surety signature. The two concepts are basically the same. In both cases, you agree to pay the debt in your personal capacity should the other person fail to pay. The cosigned loan will also appear on your credit record as you may be liable.

It is vital to check your credit record if you are acting as someone's surety. Pulling your credit record is the best way to check whether the person is making payments. If the other person has had late payments or stopped paying altogether, then it will decrease your credit score. It is better to check your credit report frequently and then talk to the other person about the late or missed payments. If the other person cannot pay you should see the creditor to rectify the problem and make alternative payment arrangements.

It is clear that checking your credit report is important for many reasons. Doing a soft pull credit check is a prudent decision to help you keep track of your credit transactions. The record will help you to identify mistakes or raise red flags for identity fraud. Remember that checking your credit record is free so do it today!

Chapter 7. The Bank Rating

All businesses need systems: systems for production, for sales, for payroll and so on. Banks are no different. And the system or process that banks use to decide which customers get the bank's money is called the Credit Approval Process.

Just like Colonel Sanders has his secret recipe for his Kentucky Fried Chicken®, banks have their own secret recipes for working out if they should lend to your business or not.

For existing businesses, banks expect to receive audited financial statements for the last two or three years as well as other internal financial reports and projections that management uses to run the business. This information is fed into a bank's internal credit rating model.

So, what information is held in a bank's credit rating model? Well, it's not rocket science. The model does a few things:

1. It produces your actual and forecast numbers in a standard format. This process is known by those working in banking as the spreading of financials.

2. It also calculates and stores different types of financial ratios for your business.

For example, the Net Income to Sales ratio is Net Income divided by Sales. The result is multiplied by 100 to make it a percentage. This particular ratio is a measure of the profitability of the products or services that your business sells.

Not all financial ratios, however, are born equal. Some ratios are much more relevant than others when it comes to deciding on the appropriate credit rating for your business.

The financial ratios that really matter when a bank works out an appropriate credit rating for your business are those that measure:

1. how well your business manages its liquidity; in other words, how well inventory, trade receivables and trade payables are managed (referred to as LIQUIDITY RATIOS),

2. the amount of existing debt in your business (referred to as EXTENT OF DEBT RATIOS), and

3. The health of the cash flow in your business (referred to as CASH FLOW RATIOS).

The assessment of the credit attractiveness of your business is based on the output from the banks' internal credit rating model. This model ranks the risk of a loan on something like a one to ten scale; a scale that is linked to a statistical probability of default and probability of loss in the event of default.
The more creditworthy a business is - measured by low leverage, high debt coverage and healthy liquidity - the better its credit risk rating will be. And the better its credit risk rating is, the more attractive the terms, conditions and pricing of the credit is likely to be.
Another approach is to use the quarterly financial statements that are substantially closer to the effective date – even if the quarter-end date occurs after the closely-held business appraisal's effective date. My rebuttal is that most information for publicly traded companies is perceptible because of information transparency in equity markets. Therefore, it passes the "knowable" test in many situations. I use this method only when the effective date and publicly traded company period-end dates are very close.

Chapter 8. How to Talk to Banks: Enter the Heads of Banks

Getting Organized

When applying for a business loan, people are often surprised about the extensive list of information that is required by the lender. This information is intended to provide the lender with details about such items as the amount of the borrower's loan request, status of the business, use of the loan proceeds, value of collateral assets, and financial condition of the business and business owners.

The size of the loan proposal will not necessarily enlarge or reduce the list of required information. The need for the lender to understand your situation, financial condition, and prospects for repayment is constant, whether the loan is for thousands or millions of dollars. The degree of scrutiny could be greater on larger transactions, but your command of this information is always important, regardless of the size of the loan proposal.

Be Prepared — Boy Scout Motto

There is no universal list of required application documents, since every deal is different. The suggested list of information presented is fairly comprehensive, but it may be either too inclusive or exclusive of items needed for any particular loan application. That's because no two loan transactions are alike — the lender, the borrower, the business, and the situation are unique in every transaction.

Hundreds of variables can change the information requirements of the lender. Even the lender will not know everything that is needed until the review process is completed.

Applying for a business loan requires you to educate the lender about the business and its owners with a customized set of standard documents, some of which are prepared specifically for each particular application. These documents will disclose a considerable amount of information from which the lender will determine whether you qualify for a loan in accordance with the lender's criteria.

In the lender's eyes, your level of preparation and degree of cooperation will be indicative of how desirable you will be as a customer. If it is difficult to get you to respond to requests for documentation and information before the loan is approved and closed, the lender will assume that it will be even more difficult to get such information after the loan is funded. When you're responsive and cooperative in meeting these information requests, you're demonstrating willingness to be part of a relationship, and you have bolstered your efforts to be seriously considered for the proposed loan.

You'll undermine the information you're providing to support your business when it contains grammatical errors, misspelled words, and incoherent ideas. With the high-quality word processing software now available you can avoid and eliminate many of these errors, even if you're not an experienced writer. There is no excuse for poorly written information communicated incorrectly and haphazardly.

When supplying information to the lender, assume that the lender does not understand the industry jargon or common abbreviations. Explain any technical terms and methodologies to ensure that the lender can follow the reasoning of your loan proposal. For example, a lender that doesn't understand how local health ordinances mandate certain minimum standards for food processing may not recognize how you can justify the costly expenditures required to build a commercial kitchen. By assuming that the lender has no familiarity with the business, your application can communicate precisely what you want to accomplish and how you propose to pay for it. Too many small businesses pay thousands of dollars annually to accountants and CPAs for the preparation of financial statements without truly understanding what this information discloses. The lender will carefully study your balance sheet, income statement, and cash flow statement. By analyzing financial trends and ratios of the historical and current financial statements, the lender will assess the financial strength of your company and will even compare it to other companies in the industry. After determining the positive (or negative) trends of these results, the lender must weigh the risks of lending money to you. The lender is primarily interested in your ability to produce future funds to repay the loan.

In addition, the lender will check your company's credit history, appraise the collateral, check references, verify account balances, and test the reasonableness of financial projections of future performance in order to quantify the risk associated with providing funding to your business.

When initiating the application process for a business loan, it is essential for you to have a detailed command of all of the requested documentation so to be ready to respond to the lender's questions and conclusions. Sometimes a business will have periods of lower performance, or other events will occur that will raise the concern of the lender. Be prepared to discuss those exceptions and to produce analysis to support the alternative explanation. By anticipating the need for these items, you can demonstrate your relevant management skills and competence in managing the business's financial affairs. The lender will need information in several distinct categories. Although there is no official format, your assemblage of documentation should be organized to assist the lender in cataloging the information more easily and evaluating it quickly. This is more efficient and in better sequence than submitting information in a business plan format.

Due to the typically large volume of material, it is more useful to arrange the information in a series of large open-ended folders, rather than using ring binders, clamps, or color-coded tabs. This system permits the lender to access and to file each section independently. Much of the information may have to be copied for various parties to review and file it, and this duplication can be done more easily if the documents are not bound in any way.

It is important to provide clean, clear documents that are entirely legible. Review everything prior to submission to eliminate incorrect compilation, incomplete pages, poor copy reproduction, or out-of-sequence documents. These logistic errors cause confusion and distract the lender from the business information you're submitting.

Never submit original documents, such as the company's various contracts. Any copied document can be authenticated, if necessary, with a dated original signature on the margin of the cover page.

Finally, if you cannot produce a particular document or other information requested by the lender on demand, it's important to provide an honest, direct explanation with a legitimate reason and a time frame for availability. If, for example, company operations are overloaded at that moment and no one can stop to prepare the information, you'll be demonstrating that the business priorities are in correct order. It is a mistake to blame the unavailability of information on the company's accountant, attorney, bookkeeper, or any other party. If you can't manage these parties (and you're the one who's paying them for professional assistance), how can you manage other operations to repay the lender's loan?

If information is not available due to reasons that cannot be resolved immediately, then consider delaying the initiation of the loan application. For example, if you're not able to obtain the most recent financial statements because the accountant has not been paid for last year's financial statement, then you're wise to wait. Your credibility would be damaged if the lender were to learn that the company's invoices are significantly past due.

Categorized organization of information will permit the lender to absorb as much or as little information as is needed. The format suggested below accommodates faster evaluation and consideration in the loan review process.

Do You Need a Business Plan?

How do companies use business plans? Too often, business owners put a business plan together only when seeking external financing from lenders or investors. Business plans should provide information on the short- and intermediate-term strategies for accomplishing long-term goals. Business plans should detail how financial, operational, marketing, and human resources will be converted into a successful and profitable venture. Business plans should be used as a road map to determine the destination and then measure results against projections.

Ensure that all documentation is easily accessed without binding or staples. Use clamps or paper clips to make lender handling and duplication easier.

Many people are obsessed with business plans — particularly those who charge exorbitant fees to prepare them. Business plans are very good tools that can assist business owners and managers to plan better and target results better. And when an existing business is seeking to obtain additional financing, a business plan can be a very good document to communicate how the company plans to build on the results they have compiled to that point in its operating history. But the plan itself is not a sufficient substitute for everything else needed by the lender.

If you've put together a business plan merely to justify financing, then it has limited utility or value for both you and the lender. If the lender requires a business plan, then you probably haven't made a clear case about what your business goals are. That being the case, you should invest the time to produce a plan. But it would also be in your interest to continue to use and regularly update the plan after the financing is obtained.

Borrower Beware!

Many lenders have had the unfortunate experience of entering into discussions with a borrower who was using false, exaggerated, or misleading information to obtain credit. Whether or not the ploy succeeded, the effects are often felt by legitimate borrowers, whose applications are subsequently scrutinized with even more diligence and suspicion. While under normal circumstances there is a natural inclination toward trusting people, lenders must be prepared to confirm everything.

Unless actual loan losses have been incurred, many lenders may be hesitant to prosecute loan applicants who have used false information to obtain their loan. But the federal government is not so hesitant, and the SBA's Inspector General is available to investigate any attempt to defraud the agency with false or misleading information. These cases are prosecuted by a U.S. attorney, who has virtually unlimited resources to pursue such matters. Most federal prosecutors have almost perfect conviction rates.

For those individuals who are flippant about the integrity of their business dealings, or who willingly try to obtain an SBA loan with fraudulent information, these actions can carry heavy penalties. It is a federal crime to submit false information in order to induce a lender and the SBA to provide business financing. If caught in such an attempt, one can be sure of criminal prosecution. If convicted, one may be punished with up to twenty years in prison and a fine of as much as $1 million plus restitution.

Business Loan Proposal

Produce information addressed to the lender that clearly sets forth the exact loan proposal you're requesting.
Many of the items listed below involve professional preparation, such as appraisals or environmental reports, which require engagement of a qualified third-party consultant. Lenders will generally approve loans subject to the information that will be provided for in these reports. You won't be required to spend any money for this information until you are assured that the loan is approved, subject to specific condition that will be confirmed by the consultants.

Chapter 9. How You Can Improve Your Credit Score

When it comes to giving advice on boosting your credit score, most people will stop at having you analyze your credit report and disputing those errors. Beyond that, the advice is usually to pay your bills on time, and don't take out too much credit. However, if you really want to improve your credit score, you'll have to be more pro-active when it comes to managing it.

This starts with gaining more knowledge about what credit really is and what it means to have it. Educating yourself is key to learning how to control better moving forward.

Most people only understand credit from the back end. They know that their credit reports can reflect negatively or positively and could be the deciding factor on whether or not they're approved for that mortgage or automobile loan. But there is much more involved than that. The more you are aware of how credit works behind the scenes, the better able you'll be to steer your own in the right direction.

When used properly, credit can be the means to your end goals. In a perfect world, you would like to see a situation where your money is put to use in an area that can help it to grow and begin to work for you. For the majority of us, working right up until the very last day of our life is not possible so when you know exactly how to use credit to help you do that, you're halfway to your goals.

Bottom line, you need to become more aware of how credit can affect your life. Ask yourself the following questions, the answers will help you to get a better understanding the role credit should play and why you need it.

Credit Habits

It may surprise you to hear that there are a lot of people that have very good credit habits but have low credit scores. It's hard to believe, but it happens more often than you might think.

There are a number of reasons why this might happen. You may pay your bills diligently for a time, but one day you may lose your job, end up in an accident, or have to deal with a major illness or other issues with you or someone in your family. When you don't fully grasp the purpose of credit, the common knee-jerk reaction is to use your credit to deal with the hard times.

This strategy may work for a little while, but as the bills begin to pile up, each month it will become more difficult than ever to keep your head above water. Before you realize it, your repayment plan begins to fail, and you're unable to keep up. The result is negative marks on your credit score.

The question then is how to create a plan that will allow you to maintain your credit health even during those hard times. Sometimes it is just a matter of focusing on not using your credit when you're not sure how to pay it back.

In general, credit is the easy fix that most people turn to when things get rough. However, if you seek out alternative options before you hit those rough patches, then you won't be faced with the need to repair your credit later. By doing this, you develop good credit habits that will carry you along even when times get hard.

When contemplating this, take the time to look back on what affected your credit score in the first place. You will usually recognize that it has something to do with poor credit habits. Perhaps you thought of using your credit cards for an expensive vacation, or you couldn't resist going on that shopping spree with your friends. Or maybe it was because something bad happened and you didn't have an alternative plan in place beforehand, and you went to your automatic relief button, your credit card. Whatever it is, in most cases, a poor credit score usually starts long before you make that first charge with how you view credit and how you handle it. Take the time to analyze your behavior towards money and credit. What do you do every day? Do you have to have that gourmet coffee on your way to work every morning? Do you have an impulse to fill out a credit application for every place you go whether you need it or not? What are your shopping habits? Are you constantly in search of a new credit card to add to your collection?

Good credit habits include more than just paying bills on time. It also includes monitoring and managing your credit on a regular basis. It involves thinking before you sign or swipe and knowing how to prioritize your finances, so you are less likely to find yourself underwater. So, rather than looking at how much you can buy and pay for, try looking at whether or not the purchase is necessary and if it fits in with your financial goals for the future.

Take a close look at your daily, weekly, monthly, and yearly habits to see where you are weak when it comes to credit management. This weakness can be identified as a credit illness, and you will have to start making plans to break that habit. Remember, your credit score is never set permanently. It is constantly changing. Even with a low credit score, by starting to practice good credit management, your FICO score will see a very fast improvement, sometimes in just a matter of weeks.

This is not to say that you can't make a frivolous purchase every now and then. We all like to pamper ourselves, buy gifts for our friends, take vacations, or provide whatever objects of desire we might want. There is nothing inherently wrong with that. However, your primary focus is to sustain your lifestyle without harming your financial image. To do that, sometimes you may have to learn to say no too many of the desirable things you want.

Take the time to look back at your credit history over the past. Identify your credit illnesses (or bad habits) that have caused your score to drop.

Creating a Plan

The way to devise a plan is to start with a clear picture of how much debt you actually have. You need to know just how much money you are paying bills every month. This list will become your primary source for payment. These are the bills that you will pay first before you make any additional purchases.

Once you have allocated and set aside money for the bills, you already have, turn your attention towards your regular spending habits. If you make a habit of writing down everything you buy and why, even the smallest item, you'll be amazed at how much money you're spending without even thinking about it. Do this for a week and then go back and review every detail. Mark off everything that you see as unnecessary and total that amount up. The result could add up to a significant amount of money. Money that could be put to much better use if you had the self-discipline to control your spending habits.

Of course, we don't want to tell you to never spend on a little extra on something, but now that you know how much you're spending in that area, you can decide just how much money you want to commit to those extras.

Remember, your goal is to boost your credit score, so that means you'll have to spend something. We've already learned that closing your account or paying off a bill doesn't really have a heavy impact on your score but spending and paying it off does. Try making small purchases each month and paying them off early. This will be a tremendous boost to your credit score. Think about using your credit card to make purchases, even if you have the cash on hand and then using the cash to pay your bill will automatically cause your score to increase. You could take this a step further by paying on your card twice a month instead of when the bill comes and see how fast your score will go up.

To be successful with these strategies, it is important that you make it a habit of documenting everything. It may seem like an extra chore, but when everything is recorded down on paper, it becomes more real than figures dancing around in your head. The physical paper actually adds another element to your credit consciousness that will serve as a constant reminder to not stray off of your plan, and it will help to build credibility with any businesses that have already extended credit to you.

What You Should Record

When you are working on revamping your habits you need to focus your attention on some very specific areas.

- Always know when a payment is due and make sure to pay ahead of time.

- Only use 30% of your credit limit. This will keep your credit utilization ratio at an optimum. In fact, try to keep your credit expenditures below that amount whenever possible.

- Never max out your credit limit. Your creditors are constantly monitoring your spending habits and will take advantage of what they learn about you. Remember, the more you spend, the more interest you will have to pay. That only serves the company and does nothing to benefit your creditworthiness.

- Use your credit card instead of cash for any purchases you make. As long as you have the money on hand to pay for it, you can be confident that you will be able to pay the bill off when it comes.

- Try to pay your bill twice a month or even weekly if possible. Your creditors will see that you don't really need the credit but are only using it for convenience.

Don't Overthink It

When all is said and done, the bottom line is it is just a matter of keeping track of the numbers. You want to make sure that you have more money coming in than going out every month. However, with most people, spontaneous spending is their downfall. So, by keeping accurate records of how much money you are spending every month, you can have better control over where your money is going.
If keeping these records feels like drudgery to you, keep in mind that the more you are aware of what is happening with your money, the more conscientious you will be about it.
It's not rocket science, but it does require commitment and dedication to make sure that you don't fall by the wayside after a bit. But what about if you don't have the money to pay for all the debt you have accumulated. What are your options then?

Chapter 10. The 7 Business Crisis Indicators

Repeating: A crisis is a situation in which, if you don't immediately deal with it and correct it, the long-term future cost to the organization will far outweigh the cost of correcting it in the present.

There are some crises in an organization that can be anticipated. These are recurring opportunities for you to manage them strategically. The difficulty is that you know in general what they are, but you don't know the time or the specific area in which they will occur. We all know we are going to have parts delivery issues; we just don't know which parts, and why it will occur. Other examples are listed below.

Operational Issues
1. Production Delays
2. Overflows
3. Equipment Breakdown

Personnel Issues
4. Product Safety
5. Organizational Integrity

Financial Issues
6. Financial — missing income numbers
7. Cash Constraints

As you look at some of these crises, which occur in any organization, you might be able to leverage them, but only if you see the opportunity that crisis can offer. Say, for example, that you are looking to replace a certain person within an organization, but they have a following or support in the organization which makes their removal more problematic. You could actually wait. There may be a crisis issue that could arise when you could then address the situation accordingly. With careful planning, you can tie that person to the crisis. For a great leader, this should be doable. Tricky, yes. During a lot of these crises, you are working to develop an understanding of what works and what doesn't work with your team. You are practicing your crisis paradigm. Why is this important? Stuff happens. Muscle memory is important.

Furthermore, there are going to be Black Swan events. Black Swans are situations in which, given history and experience, you could predict that they could happen at some point, but the likelihood is so low, that they tend to be viewed as non-existent outliers. The term comes from the belief back in the 1800s that all swans were white. But then, late during this century, a breed of black swans was found in the outback of Australia. Was the finding of Black Swan unexpected? To the Europeans—yes—but given the diversity of the world, someone should have been able to anticipate it.

Although most companies take credit for positive Black Swan events, it is the negative ones that are viewed as crises. Black Swan events are problematic in nature, because they occur outside of the normal course of business. The standard rules don't apply. Black Swan events need to be harnessed. When a Black Swan event occurs, you need to implement damage-control to work through the situation in a triage capacity. This type of crisis management is not about creating crisis, but about survival. Often it is the Black Swan event that you are preparing for when you develop muscle memory by creating a crisis; the more you condition your team to respond to created crises, the better off you will be when you encounter your first crisis outlier.

My Personal Black Swan event was when Victor Posner purchased Sharon Steel and Sharon just happened to own Brainerd Strapping. Brainerd was a well-established competitor. I was three years into my new business. I had been knocking on doors just long enough to be getting some traction. Posner purchased Sharon Steel Company and then sucked all of the cash out of it bankrupting the entire business. Brainerd Strapping was a profitable, successful business unto itself. It was pulled under and so was all of their product that they manufactured. Distributors who had been polite but non-committal all of a sudden started to call. My work that I had put forth preparing everything started to pay off.

One of the most dramatic negative Black Swan crises was the poisoning of Tylenol bottles in early 1980s. The Tylenol bottles were laced with Potassium Cyanide. Seven people died. Hard to predict. Possible yes—but no one really expected 40 years ago. How would you ever have been able to prepare your team to manage such an event? Obviously, the only thing to do is to develop the muscle memory beforehand required to react properly. This is one of the reasons why Crisis Creation can be a helpful management tool. It allows you to create connective tissue during a situation that you picked and thus control. This way, you will be better prepared for the inevitable unforeseen disaster, rather than being blindsided by a Black Swan event.

Chapter 11. Save Your Company

Stop with the New Debt

You are never going to get out of debt if you just keep adding to your debt number. It is always best to stop with the new debt and find ways to limit it as much as possible. While most people are not getting the right kind of training in how to handle money, and you may feel like it is impossible to get out of debt unless you are willing and able to go through the retraining process for your financial habits now.

So, instead of having the temptation around and taking on more debt, cut up your credit cards so you can't use them. Sit down and come up with a budget, and then stick with it. Turn on the social media and the advertisements so that they are not able to control you any longer. This helps to limit the chances when you are tempted to purchase something that you do not need.

Rank the Debt Using Interest Rates

For this one, we are going to list out all of the debts that we owe and list out the interest rate that comes with them. The highest interest rate needs to be put at the top of the list. That will be the one that you work on paying off first. Paying off the high-interest debt is going to be the key to what is known as the stack method of debt payoffs and can get that debt gone quickly.

There are other methods that work well too, but these often focus on motivational factors and can be a little bit slower at getting the work done. Interest is going to be a really powerful weapon, and right now, the banks or other companies are using it against you if you don't pay things off. Interest is going to increase the amount that you have to pay back in the end, and often we are not fully aware of how much that ends up being.

Let's say that we have a credit card that has a $10,000 limit on it, and there is 20 percent interest. You decide just to pay the minimum amount of $200 a month. In the end, it is going to take about 9 years and eight months (if you don't put any more money on it). This means that you are going to end up paying the bank $11,680 extra in just interest.

See if You Can Lower Interest Rates

In some cases, it is possible to lower your credit interest rates with the help of a balance transfer. You need to be careful with this one, but it means that you are going to move your debt to another bank, and they are going to offer you a lower interest rate to try and get your business.

If you are going to do this, you don't want just to jump right in. Make sure that you are going to actually pay the amount off rather than end up with two credit cards that are maxed out. And you should shop around to get the lowest amount of interest for the longest duration possible. Read through all of the terms and conditions that show up as well to make sure the bank doesn't have hidden fees or other issues that you need to be worried about.

Create Your Own Budget

This is where we are going to work on improving our own financial control. We need to bring out some pen and paper and write down what your total income is, after-tax, and then write down all of the expenses that we have. This includes any of the extras that you have and the minimum payments that you owe on as well.

We can then look at all of the expenses that are there and rank them based on how important they are. Look at the items that are near the bottom of that list and determine if they are worth cutting to keep you financially stable. The objective here is to create a plan where you can get the expenses lower than the income.

You also need to go through and figure out how much you are willing to spend on all of the areas of your life. You can set aside amounts for eating out, groceries, rent, buying clothes, and more. Once you allocate that money though, realize that you are not allowed to dip into other areas, and you are done at that time. You may want to consider working with a fun account that will be there just for you to spend on something that doesn't usually fit into the budget. This allows you a bit of freedom without derailing the budget.

Even if your expenses are already below your income when you start, this doesn't mean that you can just stop here and call it good. You want to make sure that you can cut your budget down as much as possible. This allows you to make more money each month and throw it at your debt payments, making it more efficient and getting that credit score in line faster than ever.

Create Your Own Repayment Schedule

The first part that we need to focus on here is covering at least the minimum on all of the debts you have. If you miss anything, even if you are trying to pay off another debt faster, you are going to incur a lot of feed and more, and these can add up quickly. Make at least this payment each month. Then, you take the debt that has the highest interest rate, and you will use the extra that is found in your budget and pay that extra towards that biggest debt. As you see, the official minimum payment goes down; you will be able to add the extra to your target debt. This will help you to really pay down the debt pretty fast, especially if you put any extra money towards that each month.

When that first debt is all done, then it is time to move on to the second-highest interest rate debt. With this one, you will take the minimum payment that you were doing before, along with the minimum payment that is available from the debt you paid off, and any extra you were paying. All of that goes towards the second debt, and that can be paid off in no time. We continue this process, taking the extras that are used from one debt and throwing them at the next one on the line, with the payments getting bigger and paying things off faster as we go along. While the first debt may take some time to complete because you are also paying on all of the other debts, but the time you get to the last few, they will be paid off in no time.

Be Kind to Yourself

Keep in mind that paying off debt, even though it is so good for your credit score, is not something that you are going to be able to do overnight. During this process, which can be a long one, you will feel that your resolve is going to be tested quite a bit. You may have an emergency that happens, like a car breaking down, and you will have to change your plans a bit.

This is a normal part of life, and not something to get really frustrated about. The important thing to remember here is not to give up and revert to your old habits, or you will never get that debt paid off. Be kind to yourself when things in life happen, but don't give up. You will get those debts paid off in no time if you are willing to do the work.

The reason that we want to work so hard at paying down our debts and making sure that they don't stick around for a long period of time is that it helps us with our credit scores while freeing up more money to do what we want. When our utilization rates are lower because we pay things off, and we don't miss payments because the amounts are not as high as they were, then our credit score will go through the roof.

Chapter 12. Learn to Build a Corporate Credit.

Here comes the fun part – the foundational steps to building business credit. The following steps will prime your business to become creditworthy in the eyes of vendors, lenders, and other credit issuers.

- The First Step: Ensure that your company name is one of a kind

Unless you have already incorporated your business, be sure that your proposed business name is not too comparable to an existing business's name. Credit bureaus monitor relationships between companies and at times apply inaccurate information to other business owner's accounts due to the simple fact that the business names are similar. So, coming up with an original business name would be a wise thing to do.

Confirm that Your Business Name is Original
 Go to the Dun & Bradstreet website and search for your company name and in the "State drop-down box, select "Nationwide".
 Confirm that your business name does not conflict with registered trademarks by going to the US patent & Trademark office website or you can pay someone to do an in-depth search for you.

- The Second Step: Pick an official office location

Vendors, lenders, and other creditors will often evaluate the quality of a business's physical address when they review credit applications. If you're starting a home-based business and want to maintain your privacy, there are ways to accomplish this. However, be sure to avoid PO Boxes and mail drops. They will likely result in a "high risk" tag on your business's credit profile.

If privacy is your concern, here are a few measures you can implement in order to minimize your exposure if your business is a home-based business:

Remove Your House from Google Maps

1. Go to Google Maps

2. Search for your home address then click on it once it appears in the search results

3. Click on the "Street View" link.

4. You will see your home on the screen. Using the "Report a Problem" link (usually located at the bottom of the screen, fill out the form on the page that follows, indicating that you want the image removed for privacy concerns. Afterwards, it should be removed.

An alternative to running a home business is to rent office space. For as little as $500 or so a month, you can rent an office at a business center and share all of the amenities. Several business centers offer short-term leases and even month-to-month leases. If you have a business that has clients come to you, renting office space may be a great move.

Note that you may need to obtain additional permits from your city, county, or state if you run a business out of a commercial office, versus a home office. Also, keep this in mind – if your business is home-based, lenders have the ability to recognize that you run it out of a home or multi-family dwelling. That isn't really an issue, but if you run your business out of a multi-family dwelling and tell lenders that your business has several employees it is likely to raise flags. Be sure to provide accurate information on credit applications to avoid heavy scrutiny over what creditors may not easily believe.

- The Third Step: Register a domain name

One of the first things you should do, even before you incorporate your business, is select and purchase a domain name for it, preferably one with the ".com" extension. It would be counterproductive to invest your hard-earned money on building your business only to find out that your ideal domain name is taken.

When registering your domain name, you want to be sure that you register one with you company's exact name or something that relates closely to it. This is because, when prospective customers discover your business by word of mouth, they are likely to search for it using your company name. For example, if your company name is Wyatt Construction Partners, it wouldn't be wise to have a domain name that says Affiliated Building.

Luckily, with the advancement of search engine optimization and other traffic generating features over the internet, you aren't as much tied down to choosing domain names that spell out your exact company name, but try to have it be a great representation of what function your business address or the name of your company.

Another reason for selecting a domain name that is easily recognized is that lenders also need to find your site at a swift tap of a few buttons. If they can't find your website through a Google search or by simply typing in your company name with a ".com" on the end, they will likely assume that your company is not well established or even worse, fictitious.

I strongly recommend using GoDaddy.com to secure a domain name. It is reasonably inexpensive and often times you can find discounts online for your purchase. Choosing this route is money well spent.

Furthermore, it is highly advisable that you invest a few extra bucks on registering variations of your company's name on GoDaddy.com. Examples of this would be MyBusiness.com, My-Business.com, MyBusinessInc.com. The reason for doing this is that you protect yourself from internet "vultures" who register variations of your company's name to steer away your customers or conduct fraudulent activity in your shadow. Protecting your company name up front by purchasing different variations of your name makes a lot of since from a business standpoint. Plus, you can actually make use of each domain as you wish – make one a page for blogs, press releases, investor dialogue, etc.

If your domain name is taken you have a few options to use…

1. Think of a new business name or alternative domain name that is still relevant to your company – If you haven't selected a name for your business yet and you're not completely attached to the one you already have, brainstorm a new name for it. If you already have decided on a business name and have it incorporated, you can still get a domain name that represents your business without using exact wording. Alternatively, you can file to "Do Business As" (DBA) which will allow you to use a different name for your business aside from the name it is registered under. This can be

accomplished through LegalZoom.com <<<ADD Off Link

2. Wait for the domain name to expire – For about $20, GoDaddy.com can monitor any registered domain name, and if it expires, they will attempt to get it for you. This typically only works if the domain name is up for renewal and its owners forget to pay the renewal fees.

3. Purchase it – In some cases, domain names are purchased but the websites associated to them are undeveloped. When this is the case, consider offering the owner of the domain name a fee to purchase it from them (around $60 and $200). You can also get a Domain Name Broker involved to handle the transaction for you if you would like to protect your identity.

- The Fourth Step – File Incorporation Documents

For the purpose of building business credit, setting up a limited liability partnership (LLC) or corporation is best since it gives your business more credibility and ensures that your personal credit is not co-mingled with your business credit. However, if you are uncertain as to which type of business entity you should use from a legal standpoint, (LLC, partnership, corporation, LLP, etc.), It is advisable that you consult a tax professional and/or an attorney beforehand.

The Fifth Step: Request a Tax ID Number
In order to establish a unique credit identity for your business, file business tax returns, and open a business bank account you will need an Employer Identification Number (EIN). An EIN is similar to a social security number for your business and it is required for corporations and LLC's. It is also needed if your company pays wages to employees.

You can get an EIN for free in less than five minutes by visiting the IRS website. When you apply for any type of business credit, always provide your EIN. Avoid using your social security number unless a personal guarantee is required.

If you'd prefer to take the burden out of applying for an EIN, we can apply and garner one for you.

- The Sixth Step: Open a Business Bank Account

Often what's most important to creditors is your legitimacy and a business bank account grant this to you.

A good place to go for a basic business account with little or no fees is Chase Bank. Their business account includes no monthly service fees if you use your debit card at least five times monthly and offers up to two hundred free transactions a month.

- The Seventh Step: Get a Business Phone Line and Stay Connected

In order to get approved for credit, your business needs to have a dedicated phone line. Lenders will verify that your business phone number is listed in 411 when they review your application. Here are a few more rules to business phone lines:
They must be 100% dedicated to business
Someone must answer the phone with a greeting that includes your company name. Alternatively, you can have a voicemail that includes all of these things

Luckily, you do not have to spend a boat load of money to get a business phone line. You have the option of either using Google Voice, adding a line to your personal cellular phone plan, signing up for a business cellular phone plan, getting internet phone service, or get a regular business phone line.

- The Eighth Step: Get Your Business Phone Line Listed in Telephone Directories

After you have setup a business phone line, you should verify that the number is listed in telephone directories such as "411". This happens automatically if you set up a business phone line through your local phone company. Otherwise, use directory assistance through the 411-call center to have your number added to the phone directory. Generally, it takes one to seven days to have your number listed. Be sure to verify that your company is listed with 411 prior to applying for business credit.

- The Ninth Step: Get Your Business Listed in Online Directories

To give your business more credibility, make sure that it shows up in the most common online directories and make business listings on Google, Bing, and Yahoo!. Doing this will also help you to get more customers contacting you for your goods and/or services.

- The Tenth Step: Create a Website for Your Business

A business website is an important resource that creditors and vendors look at to validate your business's existence. Most lenders will search your company online to verify its legitimacy and learn more about your business activities. It is wise to have a website that positively influences the opinions of vendors and creditors. Avoid simply creating a website just to take up space on the World Wide Web - creditors and vendors can spot a fraud from a mile away.

Does the sound of creating a website sound daunting and out of reach for you? If so, before you start to panic, be aware that you can create a basic, yet professional website for your business in one day for under $20-30, and without any design experience whatsoever! If you can use MS Word or compose an email, you can build a website.

Chapter 13. Free Your Mind to Free Your Company from Debt

Many folks suffer a financial crisis at some point. They may have to deal with overspending, loss of a job, a family member or personal illness. These financial problems can be and usually are, overwhelming. To make these situations worse, most people don't even know where to begin to solve these financial dilemmas. Our goal here is to shine some light on the strategies to help get youth Accumulating basic consumer debt will chain you into slavery and you could possibly spend your life held down by your own obligations to repay these loans.

Who do you work for? I don't care what you say; the real answer is your creditors if you are currently stuck paying debt. Its many forms of "dumb debt" you can get trapped into; we are all sold images and lifestyles hundreds of times per day to provoke this materialistic behavior.

What type of credit should you get? That depends on what you plan to do with the money. The most used types of credit are secured and signature credits. For smaller loans, there's no need for that, as no institution would like to end up with a store of household items, so they lend you money or issue a credit card in your name simply based on the strength of your credit so far.

There is hope; you as the borrower have many options to get rid of debt. You can take advantage of budgeting and other techniques, such as debt consolidation, debt settlement, credit counseling and bankruptcy procedures. You just have to choose the best strategy that will work for you. When choosing from the various options, you have to consider your debt level, your discipline and plans for the future.

The Good Debt

Some people find it hard to live debt free at least they will have some debt to pay off. While some debts are discouraged, good debt is considered as the money you borrow so that you can pay for things that you need or things that increase in value. On the flip side, bad debt is one that arises from things that you only want and often decrease in value.
Of course, debt isn't a bad thing; it's just how you use the money that matters.
For a good debt, you will always have a good reason to justify it, and a developed plan for paying it so that you can clear the debt as quickly as possible.
An individual with good debt will also have the cheapest methods of borrowing money. They will do this by looking at the borrowing method, rate of interest, credit amount, and charges that are appropriate to them.
Sometimes, it may imply a deal with the least possible interest rate, but sometimes, it may not.
Examples of good debt
Getting business loans. While this may not be seen as good debt, borrowing money to begin a business or expand a business is perhaps a great idea if the business is thriving. After all, you need money to make more money, right?
Sometimes, you may have to borrow capital to employ new people, purchase a new device, pay for advertisement, or even develop the first new widget you designed. The point is that you borrow this money to expand the business or increase income, then this will count as good debt.

What Is Bad Debt?

Bad debt is that which depletes your wealth and isn't affordable. Plus, it provides no means to pay for itself.
Bad debts may have no realistic repayment plans and usually deplete when people buy things at an impulse. If you aren't sure whether you can repay the money, then don't borrow the money because that will be a bad debt.

Using Consolidation or Settlement Strategies to Pay Down Debts

Debt consolidation is another strategy that can be used to manage your debts. It involves combining two or more debts at a lower interest rate than you are currently at.
But, it is worth doing your research and making some phone calls to see if there is a company that's willing to work with you. If you can lower your monthly bill to a manageable level, at an interest rate that's reasonable, that can make all the difference in handling your debt.
Like many strategies, you have had the option of settling your debts with companies for decades. Lenders always want as much money as you can give them versus being shafted for the entire amount in a bankruptcy. It is just that consolidation and settlement options rose in popularity during the recent financial crisis making it appear in more articles and news pieces than ever before.
If you have savings to pay off your debts, then start with the most expensive. Otherwise, utilize settlement options where you can reduce the amount owed if you pay a certain amount right now. As long as the account shows paid in full, with a strong payment history, your scores will increase. It doesn't matter if you needed to use debt settlement strategies to make the debt end. It just matters that you have paid the debt off instead of letting it go into arrears.

Negotiate With Credit Companies
Another thing not a lot of people know is that you can negotiate with credit companies. So you're able to take the collection letter they send you or a past due notice that has been sent to you and discuss it with them. In many cases they will take a lower amount than what's on the bill just so that they can guarantee they'll get something

Let's say you owe Discover $1,000. They want to get their money so they send you a past due notice. But for several months you've ignored that past due notice and now they've sent it to collections. The collections agency may offer you a settlement. Maybe they say they'll take $900 if you just pay it to them right then and there. You have the opportunity to call them and request that they take a lesser amount.

If you talk to the collection agency and they agree to take a lesser amount you will have to send that payment in full. Make sure that when you send them the check you write out the words 'paid in full' on the check. Make a copy of the check for your own records as well. Once they cash that check your account is legally considered to be paid in full and they are no longer able to come after you for more money.

Cut The Credit Cards
If you're looking to save some money, then you need to make sure you're spending less. That means getting rid of all those credit cards. If you're able to avoid the temptation to purchase things you can put one credit card in the back of your purse or wallet. Choose a card that will work anywhere such as a major credit card company. This is for emergencies only. An emergency doesn't mean you found something that you want to have. It means that your car broke down and needs to be towed, or you run out of gas.

The rest of the credit cards you decide to keep should be locked up somewhere in your home. Put them in a safe or lockbox. This way you have to actively think about getting the card out again before you're able to use it. This will keep you from using the card in a spur of the moment fashion and will ensure that you still have it available if necessary.

The best thing to do is make one to two small purchases on your credit card every few months. Try to space out using different cards so that none of them get taken but you don't owe very much money each month. You want to keep the amount negligible. That means its low enough that it doesn't affect your overall budget. This will let you keep the card but, at the same time, it won't completely break the bank.

Talking To Creditors

Tell them the reason why you're having a difficult time paying the debts. Most companies will negotiate a modified payment plan so monthly payments become more manageable. If you wait for the accounts to go into default, it can and most likely will affect your credit score negatively, which is what we're looking to avoid. Once in default, the collector will start calling.

Taking Advantage Of Debt Relief Services

A debt settlement company will put your deposits in a bank account, which is managed by a 3rd-party. Although you own the funds and accrued interests, the account manager will charge a fee for services because they'll be the one to transfer funds from your account to the creditors' accounts. Before signing up for a debt relief service, you must know the exact price and terms that the company offers. You also need to know how long it will be before you can expect to get results. The debt relief service firm must also inform you how much the negotiated debt is and the amount of money need to have in the designated bank account before the company can tender an offer to each of the creditors. In addition, they must inform you about the probable consequences if you fail to make the payments.

There are cases when creditors report settled debts to the Internal Revenue Service. Unless you are insolvent, the IRS may consider savings from debt relief service as taxable; meaning they may consider the situation as an income generation. As such, it is best for them to talk to an accountant. We don't want the IRS after us when we just got rid of the calls from the collection agency!

It may sound like all the debt relief companies are out to scam us, they're not. We, the consumer, just need to be aware of all the steps involved to make an informed choice about whether or not this particular option is right for our situation.

Ideally you want a company with a positive Better Business Bureau rating. You must know how much each service will cost and how long you'll have to wait to get the expected results. You should read any contract you enter into thoroughly and get every promise in writing.

Credit Counseling

Credit counseling is a service offered by some organizations to borrowers seeking advice on how they can manage their finances. It usually includes budgeting, workshops and educational resources. A counselor must receive training and certification in budgeting, money and debt management, and consumer credit. He or she must be able to tackle your financial situation and offer help in creating a personalized plan. Usually, the first session can last for an hour or more.

Chapter 14. The Typical Mistakes of a Growing Company.

1. Failing to Use Financial Statements to Manage Your Business

A sensible old sage as soon as said that if you can't measure it, you can't handle it. That declaration is definitely real in service your organization's financial declarations (the supreme in measurement) can supply all the info you require to make the finest decisions, when managing your organization. Every business transaction creates a number, and every number adds to a story that gets informed within the pages of your financial declarations. To fully understand your organization (and, in turn, effectively manage it), you definitely should understand how to compile (or have another person assemble), check out, and comprehend those monetary statements. While managing the direction of your company is definitely the most crucial usage of monetary declarations, it isn't the only one. A current Inc. magazine survey showed that 56 percent of the survey's respondents shared their financial declarations with their staff members.

Therefore, a secondary function of generating financial declarations is to utilize them to assist inform your employees on how the business works, with the underlying purpose of motivating them to do what they can to enhance success. In the event that you need to choose to offer your service, no sophisticated buyer will think about purchasing a company that doesn't produce precise and professional monetary statements.

2.   Failing to Prepare an Annual Budget.

Budgeting is among the most underrated, underutilized, and yet potentially valuable tools offered to the small-business owner. The budgeting process is a detail-oriented, tiresome discipline, and yes, it's stuffed with assumptions, however the advantages.

Precise preparation: A yearly budget is truly nothing more than a forecasted earnings and loss statement for the upcoming year. Making the necessary assumptions is always the most difficult part of preparing a budget plan. Some of the presumptions are simple to make (believe rent, office materials, and telephone services), while others are tougher (believe overall profits, gross margins, or profitability). The only way to create the best assumptions is to prepare for them, hence precise preparation is a requirement for accurate budgeting.

Expenditure control

Expenditure control is a cultural concern, and a company's culture is identified by the leader, which implies that the small-business owner is ultimately the one who determines whether or not the organization will bear in mind its costs. The very best way to start establishing an expense control culture is by adopting a zero-based budgeting system as you develop your yearly spending plan. (Zero-based budgeting methods that at the start of every year you start with zero and justify every dollar of every expenditure rather of simply including a fixed percentage.

Planning and managing expenses through budgeting not just impact success however also plays an important function in managing capital. Every dollar you save by planning to lower your phone bill collects in your examining account. You will not discover a better, or much easier, way to begin building a healthy, cash-positive service than by managing costs as long as those costs do not negatively affect your services or product, obviously.

3.   Failing to Utilize Your Certified Public Accountant. Make no error about it: Among the disadvantages of a small-business profession is that it can be among the loneliest careers. That isolation usually leads small-business owners to guide their businesses alone, as opposed to their Fortune 500 equivalents, who have their boards of directors and layers of management staffers to assist them make.

Decisions. But you do not have to go at it alone! A minimum of one individual in your working environment has the background and knowledge to assist you in directing your business; that individual is your Certified Public Accountant, or whoever prepares your organization's tax returns. What makes your Certified Public Accountant so important? Nobody can provide conclusive recommendations on how to run a service without first understanding and applying the info created by monetary declarations. Most Certified public accountants have experience dealing with other small business owners and their financial statements, most CPAs who prepare monetary declarations for small business. Owners are small-business owners themselves. Certified public accountants know how to prepare taxes correctly, which makes both you and the Internal Revenue Service delighted. While Certified public accountants don't precisely offer away their time, you don't have to give a leg and an arm to get a little consulting advice. Ask your Certified Public Accountant to tack on an hour to the end of your yearly, year-end tax evaluation.

4.   Stopping working to Understand How.

Sales is a stand-alone function, separate from marketing from the list in the preceding bullet, you can see that the "sales" activity is however one of the 9 functions of marketing.

Granted, it may be the most visible of those functions it's no more essential than any of the others, especially customer support.

5.   Hiring Too Quickly.

Why are most small-business owners so fast to employ? What makes this task so difficult? The main reason is that employing brand-new staff members falls under the classification referred to as human resources, a category that consists of tasks associated with the management of people in a company. Although you'd much rather develop a brand-new product or contact a consumer or (we hope) evaluate your financial statements, handling individuals is one of the needed evils of developing and constructing a company and hiring is a crucial element at the same time. To comprehend just how essential hiring is, attempt attaching an expense to its failure. If you work with a nonperforming staff member, the expense will equal the expense of the errors that make sure to follow, plus the expense of the left employee's lost training time, plus the time and energy needed to start the employing process all over again.

To improve your hiring skills, follow these two basic guidelines:

- *Always location employing at the top of your to-do list and leave it there until you have actually effectively accomplished it.*
- *Employ gradually. Take your time. After you make the hire, undoing it is expensive.*

6.   Taking Too Long to Terminate.

Nonperforming Employees, if we had a nickel for every time, we've heard a small-business owner state something like the following, we'd be rich! "Sure, I know it is a headache, but I can't fire the man. He's been around too long." And then, 2 weeks later he was lastly fired, and the organization is running so much more efficiently now, he would've fired him five years back." Within 30 days after working with an employee, the majority of small business. Owners can identify whether or not they've made an error. Yet, they wait another six months, or perhaps five years, to do something about it.

Businesses that do not eliminate the bad workers are at greater risk for losing their high-performing staff members to services that much better recognize and reward the best and dismiss the worst. The nonperforming employee who remains on a company's payroll not only takes excessive of management's time however likewise drags down the remainder of the group. Those workers who are performing start to feel bitter the worker who isn't performing; right after that, the group's performers likewise start to feel bitter the company owner for permitting the slacker to continue his employment.

7. Presuming Your Workers Are Inspired by the Exact Same Things You Are

Why do not my staff members do things the way I would do them?" is the normal small-business owner's lament after another employee has actually failed to solve a client's issue, neglected to act on a designated task, or eliminated of the parking lot exactly at five o'clock, leaving behind a desk stacked with incomplete work. Ask any veteran small-business owner and she'll quickly tell you that a vast majority of her work environment aggravations evolve from an inability to comprehend why her workers do what they act the method, and do they act. In other words, staff members drive small-business owner's nuts.

The primary factor for this owner/employee detaches is easy: Workers aren't motivated by the exact same things that small-business owners are. (This distinction is typically for the very best. After all, can you envision what your company culture would be like if all your employees were like you?) While the typical business owner is motivated by such things as growth, creativity, and independence, the typical worker is encouraged by such things as being part of a group, having issues solved, and sensation protected. The 2 lists are entirely different. Provided the severe difference in inspiration in between the owners of organizations and their employees, is it any surprise that workers respond to situations in a different way than their owners would choose them to respond?

To be a successful small-business owner, you have to comprehend how your workers are wired and why they do things the way they do. Then you have to make the necessary changes in your management methods to manage those distinctions. Like it or not, the burden for modification is always on you, the small-business owner, not your employees.

8. Thinking about Training Cost and Not an Investment. Envision that you own a small organization and your incomes are growing at a rate of 25 percent a year. For a lot of individuals, that sort of development would be an exciting and positive pattern, yet it can mask a variety of risks. To avoid those risks, you and your essential workers need to be growing at a similar, or much faster, rate as your organization. If you aren't, your team remains in threat of being outgrown by your organization, a situation that occurs far too often with rapidly growing small services. Go into the element of training. In fact, the dollars you invest on relevant and reliable training aren't a cost; they're an investment. They may appear under the expenditure classification on the revenue and loss declaration, those dollars could just as well be capitalized (on the balance sheet) and then composed off over a duration of time.

Chapter 15. Strategies to Solve Your Company's Crisis.

Where do I even start?
What do you want to achieve?
This is the first question you need to ask. Once you know the answer, work backward, and map out how to get there. Be strategic. It's like chess. Don't start making moves before you analyze the landscape and have a plan.
Is the issue even fixable?
If so, there may be many paths to get there. The trick is knowing which to take and with whom to take it. The best guide is someone who's been there before.
Different people have different versions of the same event. Often, the discrepancies are sincere, not biased. They're the result of fundamentally different perceptions of reality.
Have you ever heard competing versions about a breakup or other sensitive situation?
We all do it because we all have agendas. You must be able to distinguish the contradictions and understand what motivates them. If you don't, it could be your downfall.
As Eli Gold says on an episode of The Good Wife, "It's not about the facts, but what the facts can be made to look like."
Next, Answer the These Strategy Questions
How facts are presented determines how things are interpreted. What's emphasized versus what's dismissed as irrelevant? How's it framed? Was something taken out of context or a mistake printed? Did the story result from a lack of understanding?
Once you know these answers, you're better able to control the story. That's critical because what's reported by the media and written online will get read. Often by those you care about most.
Now, Drill Down Further

How deep did you step in it? How much time has passed? Is it already public? What have (or haven't) you done so far? Are you willing to bite the bullet?

What are my options?

Stopping a story from being published. If your goal is to stop a story before it's published, you need to nip it the bud.

To achieve this, you've got to be proactive and fast. Once a reporter invests significant time and it's been pre-sold to the editor, a story assumes a life of its own, and inertia takes over. Sidetracking a story requires the most nuanced work with the media. No room for clumsy actions or ill-chosen words. What strategies will resonate with the media? Can you offer the reporter a more appealing story than he has? How do you do it without offending him or making him suspect he's onto something hot?

It's not enough to just ask yourself these questions. You must know the answers and act quickly.

A large non-profit was being investigated by a federal agency. A major news organization had gotten a whiff and was snooping around. The client was terrified the issue may become public, and their dirty laundry would be aired for the world to see.

We succeeded in sidetracking the story. First, by assuring the reporter that it wasn't competitive — no other news outlets were pursuing it. This relieved the urgency. Finally, by cutting a deal with the reporter — that if there actually was an investigation (which we didn't confirm) and if it found any wrongdoing, we'd give her the complete access she desired. In exchange, she agreed to write nothing until that time.

Epilogue: Six months later, a separate problem arose, and the client's lawyer urged that we be brought back because we'd protected them so successfully before. But the client refused, complaining that we "didn't even break a sweat." Within days, the client was pilloried in the media.

That's the downside of doing a job so well you make it look easy.

Setting the record straight in the press. Your goal is to convince the reporter what "the real story" is and shift the negative tone of his coverage. Once you have his ear, use it wisely. Provide a compelling rationale to redefine the issue in your favor. Don't reiterate and respond to the allegations; that reinforces them. You're selling a different version of reality. If multiple media are covering the story, go for the most prominent. In industry parlance, that's the lead steer. Offer an exclusive to pique the reporter's interest. Other media will follow suit and try to leapfrog into the lead with fresh angles. Play that competition to your advantage, and you can control the direction of the story going forward.

Stories don't tell themselves. You've got to guide them. Unhappy with how the media is covering a story? You're not alone. Complaining doesn't help. So, find a solution. Try reframing the issue. Or clarifying the context. Or influencing the public's perception.

Journalists are drowning in work. So many stories and so little time. The last thing they want or need to do is untangle a complex issue or plow through a 40-page legal filing. Make it easier for them. Simplify the complexities, distill the legal filing, and graciously offer to guide them.

For this to work, the journalist must believe that you understand his needs, that you want to help him, and that you'll be honest or at least fair.

Softening or refocusing a story. If you can't stop a story from being published, don't fret. You have lots of tools to make it less bad.

Which to use depends on what was done, how public the issue's become, and how badly your reputation's been injured. What's the status of your credibility and reputation? Does it need protection or redemption? Can you be proactive? Make him prove the allegations. Forced to be reactive? Beware of absolute denials. Select your words carefully based on the facts.

Some routine (but threatening sounding) paperwork needed to be filed, so a subordinate did it without checking who was affected. One was a popular nightspot with a large and vocal following. The reaction was fast and furious. It became a cause célèbre on Facebook and Instagram and in news outlets large and small.

It was, in fact, a misunderstanding of what was actually happening. Could it have been handled better? Yes, and it should have. That may have avoided the problem in the first place. But that ship had sailed.

Now we needed to turn it around. That meant clarifying the context, putting it in perspective, and reassuring the public that their beloved nightspot wasn't in imminent peril. We identified and reached out to the key influencers.

Next, we saved our most powerful ammunition for the most influential news organization. After selling it on a storyline that shifted the tone, other media followed suit.

Throughout it all, only the client was visible. We provided the strategy and polished the message but remained unseen lest the public wonder why we were needed at all.

Setting the record straight online. Sometimes the battle needs to be waged online.

A daycare center gets most of its parents and students from personal recommendations. It also gets a lot through online reviews. That's why it hurt so badly when a former employee took to the Internet with negative reviews and allegations.

You must react quickly. Regardless of whether you respond publicly or privately, be gracious. If you appear defensive or petty, you'll alienate your audience.

Takedown orders are hard to obtain and can be costly. Once an incorrect story's been published online, the clock is ticking. If it's not fixed quickly, it goes in the archives, and anyone who looks you up in the future will see it. Start by explaining the error to the reporter or editor. Make it as easy as possible for them to correct. Be gracious, not threatening. If possible, provide them a graceful exit.

Generating a story. Sometimes it's to your benefit to create media attention. This is especially true in litigation if the goal is to get the other side to settle.

Warning: Two can play this game. If you think there's a chance the other side will try to do this, you need to beat them to the punch.

A prominent entertainer and golfer were in a dispute with a businessman who owned a private golf club. Not much money was involved. For the entertainer, it was the principle. So, he filed suit. We achieved extensive media coverage that shined a harsh light on the other side. Within hours after the story was published, the businessman called the manager of his golf club with a simple order: Settle this, immediately. Our client couldn't have been happier.

A legendary rock band was embroiled in a trademark dispute with a cable network but couldn't get traction. We took the fight public.

Having trouble getting traction in the media? Consider filing suit. An allegation made in a court document carries more weight than complaints made on a street corner. That aura of legitimacy can lead to news coverage that casts the other side in an unflattering spotlight — and causes them to see the wisdom of settling quickly and generously.

Of course, this works both ways. So, in a footrace to the courthouse, be sure you get there first.

How do I figure out a game plan?

The Disneyland fireworks show (really any show Disney does) is a thing of beauty. It's controlled, intentional, and carefully choreographed.

On the other side of the spectrum is a spontaneous firework show fueled by a tequila bender in Tijuana. It may sound like a good idea in the beginning, but oftentimes turns into a dangerous endeavor with less than desirable results.

The same is true for orchestrating a strategic communications plan. Lots of moving parts must mesh smoothly and precisely for the plan to work. When done well, it's a thing of seamless beauty.

A company was getting ready for a very lucrative merger. If successful, it would create one of the biggest players in the game. It was all hands-on deck for the months leading up to it. Then someone noticed a tiny thread poking out of the proverbial seam. They tugged on it gently, asking, "Hey, what's up with these accounts? I've never noticed them before."

What started as trying to trim the protruding thread quickly created a large slit up the backside of the company's "dress." If the unraveling weren't stopped soon, its unmentionables would be exposed for the world to see.

A team of attorneys was assembled to protect the company from legal pitfalls. We were brought in to manage communications and control the optics.

No two situations are identical. Neither is the response that's required. There may be a few basic similarities, but beyond that they all diverge sharply.

The most dangerous attitude in approaching a crisis is mental calcification — "I've seen this before, so I'll solve it the same way." For crisis managers, that's the quickest way to injure a client. For you, it's a fast track to missing critical details that result in hurting your business.

Chapter 16. Company Budget: Financial Indicators, Cash Flow.

If you're a cash-based business, you probably have a pretty good idea of when you make your money. Maybe your sales are highest over the weekend, or maybe on Tuesday evenings when you offer your family discount. Many businesses see a decline in income around the first of the month, when most people's rent is due – and those of you who remember when Social Security was always paid on the third might also recall a corresponding boost in business on that day and the next. When you're struggling with cash, however, you can't afford to operate on the basis of your general impressions. Tuesday may be your busiest night – but if that's only because you sell a hundred cheap scoops of ice cream to Little Leaguers after their game, then it might not be the night you take in the most cash. Maybe your income is highest on that one day a month when you offer a discount to seniors – but if most of them pay you with personal checks that won't clear your bank for several days, then you need to account for that when planning your bill payments.

In other words, you probably already know which of your sales strategies produce the most business. But you might not know which ones generate the most – or the most quickly available – cash.

Skilled financial people may choose to break down their sales and cash figures in Excel, which will permit you to quickly make calculations and comparisons that will give you the information you need. But here's a quick-and-dirty way to do roughly the same analysis without having to work with Excel or make laborious calculations.

Take an ordinary wall or desk calendar and mark two figures on it every day. The first will be your sales for the day – your accounting or POS software probably generates this information in a daily summary report, and quite likely you're tracking it already. The second figure will be the amount of cash that became available on that day – that means actual cash deposits, credit card payments that hit your account, and check deposits that cleared your bank (if your bank puts a hold on your checks). You may find it useful to round the figures to the nearest hundred or thousand, as single and double digits can present a visual distraction and aren't usually relevant for this purpose.

At the end of the month, go through and look at these figures – just look at them. Having those numbers in a grid setup should make any patterns become rapidly apparent. For instance, you should quickly be able to see it if most of your sales come in on the weekend – and whether that makes Saturday, Sunday, Monday or Tuesday your biggest cash day. You'll be able to tell if your numbers are higher at the beginning or the end of the month, or whether you have more cash sales on Fridays when many people get paid, as opposed to credit card sales which may hit your account on other days of the week. All of these observations will prove indispensable to you in determining the ups and downs of your cash cycle, thus giving you a keener edge in creating your plan.

When your firm uses accounts receivable – how to predict what you'll collect when

Firms that utilize an Accounts Receivable system generally hope to be paid in accordance with their stated terms. That is, if their terms are Net 10th, they hope to be paid by the 10th, and if they're Net 30, they hope to be paid within 30 days (see Volume 1 of this series, DEALING WITH VENDORS, for a full explanation of terms). In practice, of course, this only happens a small part of the time, particularly if those firms' customers are companies like yours, for whom making such timely payments is only a pipe dream. There are things you can do to speed up the payment process (see SUCCESSFUL COLLECTIONS, below), but if you're in a cash-poor situation yourself, you do not want to be overly optimistic – at least not when you're creating your plan. Therefore, the first step in figuring out how much you'll collect when is to determine how it has worked out historically (see AN ACCOUNTS RECEIVABLE EXAMPLE, below). Derive your estimates initially based on historical data and adjust them as needed – this will help to prevent you from being caught with your metaphorical pants down around your ankles, your empty wallet inside them.

The level of accuracy required in your estimate will increase the direr your cash situation is. A firm with comparatively minor cash flow problems may have the luxury of enjoying a margin of error totaling thousands of dollars, while a desperately cash-poor firm may need to cut that margin to hundreds, or even less. I know I've been in situations where even $50 could make a difference, and others were $2,000 one way or another wasn't that big of a deal. Likewise, with timing – you may need to count your pennies down to the day, or you may only need to ballpark how much you're going to get in a week. In general, arriving at more precise estimates is going to require more labor, so you can always try ball parking your figures in the beginning and homing in for more detail if you think it will benefit you.

Track your inflows

As with cash-based businesses, I highly recommend that A/R-based businesses make a point of tracking both their daily sales and their daily cash flow. The "calendar" method I describe above will work quite well for those who do not want to futz around with Excel. However, unlike with cash-based businesses, in which payment becomes available no more than a few days following a sale, if your firm runs on A/R, bear in mind that the time of collection is usually going to be far enough removed from the time of sale where one is unlikely to be directly traceable to the other without a great deal of paperwork. You therefore probably won't be able to see at a glance how one flows into the other, but as I discuss below, you should still be able, mathematically, to track it.

When possible, use direct tracing

Under PROJECT-BASED FIRMS, above, if your business is small enough to make it both feasible and cost-effective, you will want to plot out your projected cash inflows on a client-by-client, invoice-by-invoice, or statement-by-statement basis. Suppose, for example, that your terms are Net 30, meaning that your invoices are due within 30 days. On Friday, the thirteenth of May you send out three invoices for $5,000 apiece. Based on your historical data, you are fairly confident that of your three customers, one will pay you in four weeks, one in five weeks, and one in six weeks. You could therefore plot out your projected income schedule as follows:
Week Ending June 10th: $5,000
Week Ending June 17th: $5,000
Week Ending June 24th: $5,000

Now maybe I don't know precisely on what day these three checks will arrive, but if I'm cutting my own A/P checks on Fridays, then all that really matters is that I'm pretty sure I'm going to have that money sometime that week, which is enough information to allow me to plan.

Now suppose that instead of my invoices being dated for the 13th, they're dated for Tuesday the 10th. Well, I'm probably not going to want to change my projected payment schedule because it's likely that I will still receive those payments at some point during those weeks – in other words, they will still get rolled into that week's Accounts Payable run. If my invoices are dated for Monday the 16th instead, then I may want to push my collection schedule back a week, because I probably won't get my money until the week following – i.e., too late for the previous Friday's check run.

Now suppose that week-by-week planning isn't sufficient for some reason. Let's say I have to make an estimated tax payment on June 15th – if my money doesn't come in until the 17th, it might be too late. Then maybe I want to examine my five-week client's history more closely – do they really tend to pay me within five weeks, or is it within 32 or 33 days? Perhaps they're mailing their check out on the 30th day so I'm always receiving it a few days late (which, as I discuss in the first volume of this series, DEALING WITH VENDORS, is a strategy I myself recommend). If this is the case, then perhaps I will get their check on time, after all. But to be on the safe side, maybe I want to prioritize getting their invoice out early, so I'll have a few days leeway in case they're a little later than usual.

Similarly, suppose that with my third client, six weeks is an average. In reality, they usually pay within 40 days, but occasionally that stretches out to 49. If I'm in a position where I don't want to count on that money unless I'm pretty darned sure I'm going to get it, then I may want to push their projected payment back to the week ending July 1st. If I really need to know whether I'm going to have it the previous week, then that might warrant a polite phone call to them around the 17th to check when their payment will be going out in the current month.

You can use the same methodology for other terms, too – in fact, sometimes it's easier. If your terms are Net 10th, for example, meaning that your invoices are due on the 10th of the following month, then you will probably find that most of your customers will tend to pay at roughly the same time each month – or at least within the same week. You can therefore plot their projected payments into your inflow schedule with a fair amount of precision – these five the week of the 10th, these ten the week of the 17th, and so on. Those of your customers who are unreliable can have their projected payments shoved back to the end of the month or even into the following month, as you won't want their unpredictability to affect your short-term planning.

Firms for whom the volume of business makes this method unreasonable – or whose customers' payment schedules are too volatile to track effectively – can nonetheless achieve similar results with a little more math.

Chapter 17. Credit Risk: How to Best Manage Delays and Insolvencies

A late payment can drastically reduce your credit score and might even show up on your credit report for up to 7 years. So, stay on top of your payments and avoid any late payments whatsoever. At times, even a timely payment might inaccurately be recorded as a late payment on your credit report. If that's the case, then you must immediately raise a dispute about the same and get it removed from the credit report. If you have a history of timely payments and then end up making one or two late payments, you might probably get in touch with the creditor and request its removal.

There are two reasons why late payments are included in the credit report. The first reason is you made a late payment and that you are at fault. The second reason is you were not at fault, and the late payment is an erroneous entry. If you are certain it is an inaccurate entry, then get in touch with the credit bureau that compiled your report and raise a dispute. All credit bureaus have a legal obligation to provide true and accurate information. So, the inclusion of an inaccurate entry will not only damage their reputation but is also legally wrong.

Once you raise a dispute about a late payment, the credit bureau will look into it, and if after the investigation your claim proves to be true, then the inaccurate entry will be rectified. However, if you did make a couple of late payments, you might still have a chance to get it removed from your credit report. If this is the approach you're looking at, the first step is to make a polite request to the concerned data furnisher about the same. Try to explain your situation and make a promise to ensure timely payments in the future. There is no guarantee that this approach will work, but there is no harm in trying. If it does work, then you can successfully remove a black mark from your credit report.

Regardless of the validity of the reason why a late payment is mentioned in your credit report, it is in your best interest to ask for its removal.

If you realize there is an inaccurate entry about a specific late payment in your credit report, raise a dispute about it. At times, you can raise a dispute about the same even if you are at fault. Once again, I am stressing the fact that there is no guarantee that this method will work.

The first step is to carefully go through your credit report and identify any problems present in it. Check the credit report provided by other bureaus to check for any inaccurate entries. Once you identify the problem, get in touch with the creditor. Usually, the creditor will be more than willing to correct any inaccurate information and inform about the same to the credit bureau. After this, you must get in touch with the concerned credit rating agency about the inaccurate late payment. You are essentially raising a dispute by doing this. After you do all of this, check your credit report to ensure whether the issue has been fixed or not.

This is a time-consuming process, so, be a little patient. If the creditor immediately resolves the dispute, the process will come to an end. If you are raising a dispute with the credit bureau, it will take a while longer. It can take anywhere between 30 to 45 days. Usually, major lenders or financial institutions take prompt action when it comes to handling any dispute. If you feel like your dispute was wrongly denied or that you were doled out unjust treatment, you have a right to register a complaint about the same with the consumer financial protection bureau. Let us revisit the steps, which were explained briefly until now.

The first step is to make sure you have your credit report from all the three major credit rating agencies. If you are 100% certain about the inaccuracy of the late payment, then carefully go through the details corresponding that entry. Some details you must consider are the name of the lender, your account number, the amount mentioned, and the due date. If you're starting an online dispute, you might be provided with the list of inaccurate in entries. You might not be able to explain your story for raising an online dispute fully.

If it comes to your notice that the late payment recorded in one or more of your credit reports is inaccurate, then you must immediately contact the concerned lender or the creditor who has reported this information to the bureau. If the lender happens to be a credit card company, then immediately call the helpline number and verify the inaccurate entry. If you have used www.annualcreditreport.com to obtain your credit report, then the information about the concerned lender who reported the entry will be mentioned in the report. It is your immediate duty as well as the responsibility to notify the lender about the error immediately. If it is a genuine error, the lender will act promptly and take the necessary steps to fix it. At times, you might also be asked by the lender to provide proof of the timely payment you make. You can use your bank statements or any other supporting document to provide the required proof. If the lender is satisfied with the proof you furnished, they will take steps to fix it.

If the lender agrees about the inaccuracy of the entry made, then get the confirmation about the same in writing. It is always better to have a written verification because if the lender disputes your claim in the future, you will have proof on your side. Once the lender has accepted the error, he must inform the credit bureau about it as well. If you want, you can always approach the credit bureau directly and raise the dispute. If you ended up paying any late fee or penalty due to the inaccurate reporting, you could claim reimbursement for it from the lender or creditor. If this doesn't work, and the lender denies the dispute even when you are right, contact the credit bureau immediately.

The credit bureau can take anywhere between 30 to 45 days to verify your claim and revert their findings to you. You might have to submit all the required proof to support your claim while doing so. Feel free to raise a dispute online, through the mail, or even via the telephone. If the investigation proves that there was no error, then the credit report will stay unchanged. However, if there is an error, you will receive a free copy of the updated credit report.

You can follow the steps only when you're not at fault. However, what can you do if you are at fault? You might be able to get the late payment removed from your record, but the chances are quite slim. It might not necessarily happen, but what's the harm in trying? While doing this, don't try to lie your way out of it. Keep in mind that the electronic systems used for verification are quite accurate these days. The lender might take a while to verify your transaction, but you cannot get away with it. Making any false claims will worsen your relationship with the lender and might also close any existing lines of credit you have.

You can try negotiating and convincing the lender for the removal of the late payment. To do this, keep in mind you will have to do a lot of negotiating and come to an understanding. There is no guarantee this can walk. The lender has no obligation whatsoever to meet your request. So, try making an honest appeal to get the negative remark of your credit report. For instance, if there was some technical error, which prevented you from making the payment on time, you might be able to explain your situation to the lender. Or perhaps there might have been certain unforeseeable conditions that prevented you from making the payment. Regardless of the reason, if it is an honest reason, you might be able to convince the lender to change the entry.

Avoid Late Payments

When you make a late payment, you will not only have to pay a fee or a penalty, but it will also harm your credit score. A couple of late payments means you will not be eligible for lower rates of interest and might end up paying high rates. Also, if you're late on a payment by more than 30 days, it will show on your credit report and will stay there for seven years. So, it is a good idea to take steps to prevent making any late payments in the future. You must do this, especially if you're trying to improve your credit score

Auto pay

Perhaps the easiest way to avoid any late payments is by automating your payments by signing up for a service like autopsy. By doing this, you are essentially authorizing a credit card issuer or a bank to make automatic payments for certain monthly expenses on time. You can use this service for automating monthly utility bills to avoid any late payments. Before you sign yourself up for any of these services, ensure that you have sufficient funds in your account if not automatic payments will not be possible. Also, check if any fees or charges are applicable for using such services. Timely payments will help improve your credit score in the long run.

Reminders

If you aren't too keen about automating any payments, ensure that you pay all your bills before the due date. You can set reminders on your smartphone or even maintain a journal to do the same. There are various online services you can use to set reminders about the same. Also, financial institutions that have given you loans will also provide online reminder services. So, contact your bank and enroll yourself for their online alerts.

Weekly payments

Another simple technique, which you can use to ensure prompt and timely payments, is to divide your payments and pay them on a weekly basis. Make a list of all the expenses at the beginning of the week and ensure you clear them by the end of the week. This is a great way to start budgeting and managing your finances. You can develop mindful financial habits by doing this. If you know that you are required to make certain weekly payments, you will become conscious about your daily expenses.

Call your lender

If you missed any payments, you must immediately make the payment and then contact the lender. Try to take action as quickly as you possibly can to remedy this situation. As mentioned, even one late payment can cause significant damage to your credit score. If you have a good track record and have been punctual customer, the creditor might be willing to waive off a single late payment. However, don't make a habit of making late payments regularly.

Chapter 18. Financial Planning and Financing Requests: You Decide the Conditions of Your Financing

As a prelude to developing pro forma projections and cash flow forecasts, it's important to form judgments about a company's health and its related potential of future earnings. Financial planning has a long history. It goes back to War II when they were developing the project management processes — from taking a plan to implementing, monitoring, and improving it. That's the typical project management process. In the financial planning world, you begin with establishing the relationship and gathering data. Technically, as a lawyer and a wealth manager, I would sit down in the data-gathering process and go through things with each client or each family. The data-gathering process begins with questions like the following: Where are your investments? What are your assets? Do you own a home? Do you own a second home? Do you have a retirement plan in place? Do you have insurance policies in place? What is your family dynamic? Are you married? Do you have alimony? How many kids do you have? All of these things are part of the data-gathering process.

The importance of financial planning is not in the preparation but in the interpretation and the analysis. That comprehensive and intelligent presentation of information are the components of analysis and interpretation which would help those who are concerned in making a judgment and the right choice. Interpretation means explanation, understanding the significance of a data in a very simplified manner. Interpretation includes the making of conclusion, profitability, financial soundness, as well as the efficiency of a business. It is an art which requires so much more than arrangement and analysis. Interpretation is quite different from analysis, and they are related. However, you can't make an analysis without interpretation because the data of financial statements are not uniform or entirely the same. That is why analysis requires you to reclassify, re-arrange, and make that connection between them. Interpretation is at that conclusive stage, which is performed through that process of comparison. Sometimes we can say that both analysis and interpretation can be the same thing.

Analysis and Diagnosis

The next phase of the financial planning process is analysis and diagnosis. Just like any doctor or lawyer, if a client or patient comes in, they're going to explain what they have or what's going on, and then you are going to begin the process of diagnosis and analysis. You're looking at all of the investments and assets, the retirement plans that they have, and their estate planning issues. You will be analyzing with regard to the client and his or her family and family dynamic. You will be trying to piece it all together so you can put together the best plan and the best suggestions for this particular client.

Establishing Objectives

This section is the actual plan and putting it together. You might think, "How do I put together a plan? Do I use certain software or a certain product?" There are hundreds of companies out there that sell financial planning software. The company that you work for might be using either a proprietary set of software or something they have purchased for use. That software, believe it or not, will allow for inputs. It will ask you questions: What is the home worth? What is mortgage on the home? What is the interest rate? What is the pay off? The next page might have input data fields for what your 401(k) looks like and its value, how much you contribute to it every month, and so forth. The next page might ask if you have any insurance, like life insurance or disability insurance. Each part of your financial background is really a different section of the plan, but it intermingles with the other parts of the plan in total. If you're not using software, you could technically work on it by yourself. Some people at home might be using just a proprietary plan that they downloaded online or something from one of the big companies like TurboTax. These are some examples of how planning is done, but in the wealth management world, typically, they provide wealth management financial planning to some of the wealthiest customers at the individual firm. The planning systems they have in place are usually high-caliber software. The planning aspect is really piecing together each aspect of the data into different subsets, whether it be investments, estate planning, or tax planning, and then putting something together that you can actually present to an individual or to a family. In that presentation, you can address all the issues and recommend suggestions to be implemented.

Implementing Plans

The implementation of the actual financial plan is sometimes the hardest part because you're usually working with an individual who is wealthy or successful, and you're asking them to take action or to do something. Sometimes you can't make anyone do anything, but you can make all the suggestions and explain to them how it might save them in the long run, help them make or save money, protect their business or their income, or even protect their children. The implementation of the plan is challenging. You can present everything to your clients or to the family and say, "This is what I would do if I were you, and this is what the tax lawyers say is the best thing to do." What the investment guy says is "This is the best thing to do." Some products and services that we offer can supplement your actual situation. That's what happens typically in plan implementation. With a large firm, you usually are going to be making proposals and recommendations that allow you to sell your products and services. It's not unethical to do that at all because these clients can go out and buy those products and services wherever they want. You are just saying that you've done the financial plan and the wealth management analysis, and you have some recommendations: Here's what our products and services look like and how they can help you in the long run.

Chapter 19. Company C.V: How to Present the Company to the Bank.

Every serious business must have a business plan also known as a CV. Even if you've managed to be somewhat successful, you'll need a business plan when you decide to expand. It highlights key aspects of your business and is required by financial institutions. At a minimum, a business plan should include 5 years of projected growth. Here is an example of page one and the table of content followed by a breakdown of the various sections that constitutes a business plan. All sections do not have to be exact however all aspect of the business must be captured in your plan.

1. Cover Letter

This is the first section of the plan. An established business will have a much more detailed plan however this is for a new business. Include the dollar amount that you intend to borrow, duration and terms of the loan, type of funding you want.

2. Executive Summary

The summary gives the reader a quick picture of your entire plan. It should include business name, location and description, products/services, market, competition and management qualifications. Business goals should be clearly stated. Be sure to list any financial needs and how funds will be allocated to each need. Finally, state expected earnings and how it will be disbursed to investor.

3. Market Analysis

Everyone must do a market analysis of some sort before launching a business. Included in your analysis should be industry and market description with size, trends, geographic considerations, competition and pricing.

4. Products/Services

Give the reader details of your products and/or services. Be sure to include a description of products or services and how it will benefit consumers. It is important to address patents and other legal or technical factors. Compare and contrast your products/services in respect to that of your competitor. Include manufacturing procedure if applicable.

5. Marketing and Sales Strategy

Define how you intend to market your business. List the overall marketing strategy in terms of sales. Showcase your pricing policy in this section and list the terms of sales. Be sure to list your plans for distributing, selling and servicing.

6. Organizational and Management Plan

Specify the unique style of your business in terms of organizational and management plan. In other words, show the form of business organization you have including directors or officers if applicable. Include organizational chart with each member's defined responsibility. Having each key personnel resume as part of this plan is also a good idea. List plans for staffing and payroll with detailing number of employees as well as cost. Any facility and operating plans for the next 5 years should be listed. Be sure to address any government mandate that directly affects your business.

7. Financial Data and Projection

It is critical that all borrowers have a financial projection. No financial institution will lend your business money without it. A five-year financial history and projections including profit and loss statement, balance sheet, cash flow and estimates for capital expenditure must be listed. Be sure to explain your projections and use of funds and include factors such as key business ratios. Conclude with graphs and charts to illustrate positive trends and list expected returns for investors. Imagine owning several businesses that generates a million dollars each and every year. Now that you've visualized the idea, it's time to make it a reality. It is really not difficult to be successful in business, just intelligence and persistent. There aren't any limits on ventures that yields attractive returns when you position yourself appropriately. For the same reason, you may see a successful business somewhere but an unsuccessful one of the same types elsewhere. What and how it is operated can make or break it. I'll list a few diverse and known profitable businesses models to give you some ideas. Although these businesses tend to do well, I'm going to show you one or two additional unique selling proposition (USP) to make you stand out and attract relatively more customers.

Business Center Model

This business consists of having a brick and mortar storefront where customers can print, make copies, fax, and access the internet etc. for a fee. Other services that should be incorporated into the print shop are ink/toner refills and being USPS, FedEx, and UPS authorized shipper. Add a small section for mailboxes. Many home and businesses will rent the mailboxes because they don't want to make their home addresses public. Be sure to sell all related stationery as well since some of the people that visit the store may need such items. Just look at the demographics of consumers that will frequent your store if you cater to their needs. For instance, clients may want phone cards and cell phone accessories as well as gift packaging materials.

Apart from selling a long list of related items, you'll generate income from the core services of printing therefore this business should not be overlooked. Location is a very important factor to consider. Construct your business in a highly populated area that has no such services to enjoy a great return on your investments. Your unique selling proposition (USP) could be having express designers on demand. These designers can handle anything like websites, logo, video production, graphics, marketing materials, writing, programming, voice over and sound effect etc. Your business can contract these services from several reputable online services and charge a markup. You are basically outsourcing these USP's for a profit.

- Merchant Services Model

When you operate a merchant services business, you can incorporate other services such as security and alarms. Here is the breakdown of the said model. Virtually every business has to accept payment through a variety of methods other than cash. Merchant services provide credit/debit card terminals and accessories. An attractive means of profit will also derive from the sales of security cameras and monitors. Secure a contract with ADT, the largest company of its type in America and you'll get several thousand dollars per customer sign-up. As you can see, a firm like this is extremely lucrative with multiple streams of pulling revenues. Move in quickly on new businesses before your competitors do, for they are your primary target. That said, be sure to obtain a listing of all new business fillings from your state. Hire a telemarketer from oversees to offer your services to these businesses. You can find many telemarketers online that speaks English, Spanish, and several other languages. They are usually managed by a company that provides the facility and charge them a fee. Since this is a business to business services (B2B), your USP could be the service of telemarketing which you can attain from your oversee source. Offer all your business customers a telemarketing service for a fee.

- Cleaners Model

What comes to mind when you hear the words laundry mart? Perhaps you may think of a place where people go to wash their clothes and other washable belongings for a fee. You are absolutely correct, and you can expand your investment into this area for higher profits. This business requires very minimum staffing when compared to others. Establishing a laundry mart is all about location. Set it up in a heavily populated lower income residential area and you'll get all the business you can handle. Your rent or mortgage should be relatively lower as opposed to a middle-class neighborhood.

Please keep in mind that modifications to the plumbing and electrical systems will have to be made if you lease a building. Washers and dryers should be purchased with an extended warranty that covers repair or replacement option plan. This way, you can avoid costly repairs after the initial manufacturer's warranty. Pick up the money generated each day and deposit it into your account and within a short time you'll see the value in this business.

As you cruise through the middle-class sections of your town, you see people paying for convenience. It is true that people pay for services that they cannot do or just don't have time to do. For majority of the professional workforce, washing their own clothes and ironing them is a bit of an inconvenience. They prefer to drop off their dirty garments and uniforms at the dry cleaners early in the morning before work, then pick it up later in the afternoon after work. People that take their apparels to the cleaners do it in bulk and do so on a consistent basis.

Dry cleaning is very much another viable and profit pulling business that can be tapped into. You can even own and operate this service without having the washing machines at your physical location. It is a practical alternative that many owners are now doing however you'll generate more income with your own equipment. Simply sub-contract with a cleaner and drop off your load in the morning at 10am, then pick it up by 4pm the same day. If calculated correctly, customer who brings their items by 9am can get them back after 5pm on the same day. Most customers will not know nor care that their items are being remotely cleaned. Your USP could be marketing to large firms to pick up their laundry at work in the mornings and delivering them in the evening. It is a convenience that many people would enjoy as its one less stop for customers and it saves them time.

- Education/ Care Model

Do you know that with just 50 customers all paying you six hundred dollars a month equals thirty thousand dollars a month? Of course, you do, and if the total cost of running the business a month was twenty thousand dollars, you'll earn ten thousand dollars a month in profit. Calculate and you'll get one hundred twenty dollars a year. I must admit, I'm being modest with these numbers because it can quickly double, triple or even quadruple with proper planning.

The subject at hand is preschool/childcare services. It includes full time care, before/after school care, preschool curriculum, tutoring, homework assistance, and physical activities such as karate and dance lessons. Hire qualified care attendants and a program director. Establish a contract with a tutoring, karate and dance studio to have an instructor come in 3 times a week to teach. Coordinate so the instructors are able to use the same room but at different times with just a few quick modifications. Charge parents' additional fees for the extra services. Many will be happy to participate because it will help their children's development.

This model can be adopted by anyone who has the ability to employ the educators needed to provide the services. Requirement varies from state to state with a common denominator being background check since they'll be working with children. Qualifications that should be stipulated are prior experience and CPR certification for care attendants and director current certification status for the program director. Thorough research is the key to success in this model. Secure a good location and a very good preschool curriculum.

Chapter 20. Real and Personal Guarantees

What is going on in the credit card industry? At a time of global economic slowdown, the credit card companies are snatching the benefits from their customers by lowering the cash and credit limits for their cards, upping card fees and reducing reward programs, resulting in a reduced interest in plastic money dealings.

When the storm named 'recession' struck the global corporate world, the effects were severe for numerous domestic and multinational companies in the U.S. and the entire free world. This became the major reason why the card companies and banks were forced to lower the credit and cash limit of their plastic money products and also start taking the dark steps of cutting the discount offers which benefited the customers and attracted them towards the plastic money culture.

Some banks have also slashed the cash limit for its users and borrowers. However, the banks have taken this initiative by looking at the credit repayment and total income record of the individuals, which means that those individuals with a solid credit history a good job need not worry. Right?

Many banks have slashed the credit and cash limit, but some major banks are still continuing on with the discount schemes they used to provide before the economic slowdown hit. If the slowdown continues to disturb the business atmosphere of the world, it will surely reduce credit card usage and significantly impact the plastic money business.

For a newly established business without corporate credit, receiving approval for a business credit card would be impossible; the only alternative would be the business owner's personal credit history. If you carefully examine these contracts, you will find that they contain a clause that discusses your personal liability as the owner of the business credit card account. What does the personal liability provision mean and how should this affect you?

When there is a personal guarantee on a business credit card agreement, you are agreeing to guarantee the account personally. This means that in case the business fails, and repayment becomes difficult, you – the business owner – are personally liable to pay off all charges in your business credit card.

TIP: If the application asks for your social security number, you are not applying for a true corporate card!

Under the personal liability clause, the cardholder's personal credit history can be damaged if there are unpaid charges on the business account. If your company incurs a large amount debt, your own credit rating can drop, even if you don't have any problem with your personal accounts. As the owner of the business and the owner of the business credit card, you are directly responsible for this account.

Avoiding Personal Liability

Is it possible to be free from the personal liability clause? The answer is yes. If you have been using your business credit card for at least two years or more and your record shows that you have been a consistent player, you can request your business credit card company to remove the personal liability provision. Still, the decision will depend on your business credit card issuer and the card is not a real business credit card.

Earlier I recommended that you register your company with D&B and Experian. By signing up with D&B and Experian you can apply for a business credit card as soon as you create a positive credit history. Once you have a true corporate card it will help you start building your business credit more easily.

Be sure to select a business credit card that will report your payments to the business credit reporting agencies, not to personal credit reporting agencies. Building up your corporate credit may take some time, so establishing a business credit card account as early as possible can work to your advantage. Remember, separating your business and personal credit history does not mean you should be careless in managing your business credit card. It is still important that you watch your credit card use, stay within your credit limit and submit your payments on time. By doing this, you can be sure that you'll maintain an excellent business credit standing.

Chapter 21. How to Protect Your Credit?

Having credit available to your business in the form of loans, lines of credit, and credit cards, while maintaining your business credit rating means that...

- The cost of doing business will be less. You will pay less for insurance, rent and equipment leases, interest on loans, and more.

- Vendors will extend credit to you for things like inventory purchases. This will allow you to keep as much cash in your business as possible and not "tie up" funds unnecessarily in inventory or raw materials.

- You will be better equipped to weather financial storms through the use of your credit.

- You can hold onto as much of your cash as possible and leverage your credit for the growth of your business.

So, what is this "credit" that you'll be leveraging? It is essentially the reputation of your business, or your financial history, which in turn makes your business a trustworthy candidate for loans and financing. In other words, by building "credit" you can make the most of your financially responsible past.
Let's talk about how exactly you might do that.
Leverage
Let's first talk about what we mean by leverage.
Leverage is defined as "the power to act effectively", and in the investing world leverage refers to the practice of investing with borrowed money.

When I use the term leverage, I am generally referring to one or both of these meanings. Let's talk about each of them and how they apply specifically to your business and your use of business credit.

The Power to Act Effectively

Business credit gives business owners the power to act effectively. You are not limited by what's in the bank account on any given day. You have the power to invest and act in ways that will accelerate your business's growth and maximize your profits.

Here's an example of what I mean:

Bob the business owner has spent the time, money, and energy necessary to build a solid business credit profile. Bob the business owner doesn't know it, but his company is about to hit a major roadblock.

A major supplier unexpectedly closed up shop and left a large hole in Bob the business owner's supply chain. Luckily, Bob had great business credit established and so he was in a position of leverage. Bob was in an ideal position to handle the stress and difficulty of this situation. Bob had within his grasp the power to act effectively. Bob used his excellent business credit rating to quickly get accounts set up with new suppliers to fill in the gap left by the defunct supplier. All is well with Bob's business as a result.

Simply having a strong business credit profile with good cash flow, net worth, and business credit scores can give your business the power to act effectively in a wide variety of situations.

Investing with Borrowed Money ("Leverage")

When referring to the word's use as it relates to general investing, leverage typically refers to the practice of investing with borrowed funds.

Here is a simplified outline of what leveraging might look like in an investing context:

An investor has $5,000 cash to invest.

- The investor wants to invest in a particular company.

- The investor uses margin investing (leverage) to purchase $25,000 worth of stock instead of only $5,000.

- The price of the stock increases over time by 20%.

- The investor sells the stock and collects the $5,000 (20% of $25,000) return on their investment.

- The investor has doubled their cash and now has $10,000.

This is an over simplified illustration, but hopefully you get the point. The idea is that a $5,000 investment wouldn't double nearly as quickly on its own, but if you use leverage to make it a $25,000 investment, it has the potential to do a lot better a lot faster. The downside to this, by the way, is that the losses associated with margin investing can exceed the cash investment amount. So, if things hadn't gone so well, our investor above may have lost $15,000 instead of gaining $5,000. It is for this reason that margin investing is considered risky and its use is usually limited or restricted in some way.
Here's how this applies to your business with another simple example:

Let's say you have $25,000 cash available (in the bank) to use in your business, and your current cash flow is in the positive with $5,000 each month coming in above your current expenses. You need cash to operate your business so you can only spare about $10,000 of your available cash for a big marketing campaign. You have tested this marketing approach and you know that for every $5,000 you spend; you can expect $8,000 worth of business to come in the door. If you choose to use your $10,000 cash, you can expect to generate $16,000 in business, but then you will have exhausted your cash. You consider using your available cash flow to fund the marketing campaign, but this would bring your monthly cash flow to zero, which isn't a good place to be. Instead, you decide to leverage your business credit and finance a larger version of the marketing campaign. You invest $30,000 into your business to fund the marketing campaign using your business credit and hold on to your cash. You use your existing cash reserves to make smaller payments on the $30,000 credit line while you wait for the marketing campaign to pay off. Once the campaign is complete you've brought almost $50,000 of new business in and only used around $4,000 of your available cash (for payments on the credit line, over time) to make it happen. You pay off the loan and re-invest the remaining revenue into your business.

In this simplified example, we can see that investing in your business with borrowed money works similarly to investing in stocks with borrowed money except you can minimize your risk since you're the one running the business! You know your numbers. You know what you're capable of. If there is an operation which needs financing (especially one with a direct payoff such as a marketing campaign), business credit is often a powerful way to finance the undertaking without draining your cash.

Investing in your own business with borrowed money (using your business credit) is like taking every dollar that you have to invest and multiplying it by 5 or 10, and then putting THAT resulting pile of money to work in your business.

Using strategies such as this, it is possible for businesses to maximize their growth potential.

Applying business credit to your business

Using this and similar approaches, you can probably see the power of leveraging business credit in your business. Whether you choose to use business credit for growing your business faster, or for making the ride smoother along the way, the effects can be powerful.

The smartest and best way to use business credit is the way that will benefit your business the most. Consider your own business, finances, sales numbers, forecasts, and cash flow. Where might you leverage the power of business credit to make the most of your available resources?

The possible answers to this question will vary substantially from business to business. It depends on what stage your business is in, what your outlook is, what your goals are, and more.

With the right mindset, some legwork to get your business credit in order, and a little planning, the sky is the limit.

Chapter 22. Corporate Loans: There Are Not Only Banks

Starting up a business requires start-up funds. If you have your own savings prepared for your venture, you likely will not need any funds for a while. Still, it is important to know what is available to you in case this becomes something you need to take advantage of in the future.

There are many routes you can go when it comes to requesting or receiving funding for your business. What venture you go will heavily depends on what you are trying to accomplish, and what amount of funds you need.

Online Lenders

Online lenders are growing in popularity and are a great alternative to business loans through the bank. Many different online lenders are willing to lend to the majority of people. Simply go online, choose the one that best suits your needs, complete the application, and wait for a response. Depending on what online lender you look at, you may receive your response instantaneously. Otherwise, you will receive it within a matter of days. Online lenders are typically fast as well, issuing funds often within just a few days of applying.

Angel Investors

Angel investors are individuals who help start-up companies on a regular basis. The typical agreement when receiving investments from an angel investor is that they receive 20-25% return on their investment. One great aspect of having an angel investor on your team is that they are typically highly experienced with start-up businesses, and they can bring a unique skill set to the table to help you advance your company quicker. If you choose one properly, they may become both a financial asset to your business, as well as a skills-and-knowledge-based asset, too.

Venture Capitalists

Venture capitalists are similar to angel investors, except that they have no desire to be involved in the business itself. They will provide you with the investment funds, granted they agree to invest in the first place, and then they will expect you to continue with business as usual. It is a more hands-off approach to having investors. However, something to consider is that venture capitalists do still have a percentage in your company as long as you have their investment, so they can speak up whenever they desire, and based on the percentage of the company they currently hold, can have a significant influence on your business. For this reason, it is important to ensure that you choose an investor who will align with your business goals and needs, and whom you can trust.

Grants

Many businesses are eligible to receive grants from the government. Small business grants enable small businesses to receive funds for fitting into a certain sector of the economy. Essentially, as a small business owner, you gain access to these funds for fulfilling a role in the overall economy. Each locale has a different selection of grants available to them, as does each industry, and sometimes even each niche. It is important to check into what these are for your own locale so that you can access any grants that may be available to you!

Chapter 23. Crowd Funding and Other Non-Bank Loans

As you've heard many times, it takes money to make money. To get your new business up and running, you need access to money, usually referred to as start-up capital or seed money. This is the money that will be used to pay for leasing office space, buying necessary equipment, acquiring necessary licenses and permits, hiring your first workers, producing your products or acquiring inventory, marketing, and all other expenses associated with starting a new business.

In an ideal world, an entrepreneur will have enough money saved up to fund their new business. Even though some entrepreneurs do fund their new ventures with nothing other than their personal savings, this isn't the case for everyone. Starting a new business, as any logical individual would know, requires money. So, how do you finance your business if you're starting from zero?

Below are several approaches you can use to raise start-up capital:

Borrow Money from Friends and Family

This is a very common way of raising startup capital, and also one of the easiest. According to a joint study by the Kauffman Foundation and Babson College, London Business School, 70% of all capital investments in start-ups comes from friends and family.

With this approach, you simply need to talk to some of your friends and family, tell them about your business idea, and ask them to loan you some money to fund the idea. The best part about this approach is that you won't be asked to fill endless paperwork or go miles to prove the viability of your business idea.

While it is the easiest, this approach is also one of the riskiest. If you get start-up capital from your friends and family and your business fails (which is a possibility for every new business), you will not only be risking your loved ones' financial future, and you will also be risking your personal relationship with them.

The best approach when asking for startup capital from friends and family is to treat it with the same seriousness you would when borrowing money from an investor. Go over your business plan with them and show them your projections to provide evidence that you are not just sinking their money into a stupid venture. Clearly state the terms of the arrangement (is it a loan or an equity investment?), and how you intend to repay. Finally, remind them that there is risk involved, and that they could potentially lose their money.

Use a Credit Card

Credit cards are another easy way of raising money to fund your new business. According to a survey by Arthur Andersen and the National Small Business Association, about half of all small business owners have at one point used their credit cards to fund their business' formation or expansion. Used responsibly, credit cards can be a great way to pad your finances when your cash flow is low.

Unfortunately, with ease comes risk. Credit cards have some of the highest interest rates, and if you are not careful, using credit cards to fund your startup could land you in a hole of debt that might take you years to get out of. Aside from the high interest rates, the penalties are numerous and high if you miss any payments.

If you decide to use credit cards to fund your business, have separate cards for personal and business expenses. The credit card interest charged on business expenses is tax deductible and keeping your personal and business expenses separate will make it easy for you to claim these deductions.

Use Funds from Your 401(k)

Many people are not aware of this, but you can actually use the money in your 401(k) to fund your business. To do this, however, you need to follow the right procedure, otherwise you might face hefty penalties.

Tapping into your 401(k) to fund your business involves some legal complexities, including setting up a C corporation that has a retirement fund into which your retirement assets can be rolled. To avoid falling on the wrong side of the law, it is advisable to have a CPA, a tax attorney, or someone well versed with establishing C corporations handle this for you. The person should also be highly knowledgeable about the Employee Retirement Income Security Act (ERISA).

When funding your new business using the funds in your 401(k), don't forget that you are taking a double risk. If the business fails, you lose the business as well as your retirement nest egg. Therefore, it is advisable to minimize your risk by not using all your retirement funds.

Crowd fund Your Business

The ubiquity of the internet has led to the growth of unconventional ways of raising funds for a new business. Crowd funding is one of them. With crowd funding, you basically pitch your business idea to people on the internet, let them know how much money you need, and then ask them to contribute money to your idea. If they like your idea, people will give you money to implement it, in exchange for something, such as getting your product once your business is up and running.

There are several sites where you can crowd source money to fund your idea. The most popular is Kickstarter.com. Ever since its inception in 2009, Kick starter has successfully funded over 176,000 projects and raised over $4.7 billion. Other popular crowd funding sites include Indiegogo and GoFundMe. GoFundMe is more geared towards social causes and unfortunate life events, but you can still find people to fund your business idea on the site.

If you want to raise enough money for your start-up through crowd funding, you need to tap into your social network. Remember, there are thousands of other projects vying for the same crowd funding dollars as you, and therefore, your chances of hitting your target are higher when you rally up strong support from your followers on social media. This means that you will need to do some marketing to get more people to support your idea.

Get an SBA Loan

The US Small Business Administration (SBA) is a government agency that provides guarantees for loans by financial institutions to small businesses that cannot ordinarily access loans from these financial institutions. The SBA itself does not offer loans. Instead, it guarantees the lender that it will pay the loans in case the small business is unable to pay the loan. There are some conditions that you need to meet in order to qualify for an SBA loan. These include:

- You need to have applied for a loan from a financial institution and got turned down. The SBA only guarantees small businesses that cannot obtain loans on their own.

- Your business needs to fit the government's definition of a small business. This definition will vary depending on the industry you are operating in. Some industries are judged based on number of employees, others on annual income, and so on.

- Your business will need to meet other qualification requirements based on the type of loan you are applying for.

After meeting the above conditions, you will need to apply for a loan from a bank or financial institution that offers SBA loans. Remember, the SBA doesn't offer loans itself. You will need to pass the bank's qualification requirements in order to be approved for the loan.

Below are some things you need to do to increase your chances of qualifying for an SBA loan:

- Make sure you have a good credit score, preferably in the high 700s and above.

- Have a business plan ready, detailing what business you want to get into, why you need money, and how you will ensure the success of the business.

- If you are borrowing money to fund the growth of an existing business, you will need to have a complete financial history of your business. However, since you are starting a new business, this is not necessary.

- Have financial projections ready to show that your business's ability to pay back the loan.

Get a Microloan

Microloans are small business loans offered by micro lenders. Microloans typically range between $500 and $35,000. The good thing with micro lenders is that they give loans that are way smaller than banks would give you, have more flexible underwriting criteria, and don't need as much documentation as banks. A microloan can be the perfect way to fund your business idea if you are unable to raise funds through a bank loan.

Microloans have several advantages, including:

- They give very small loan amounts, so you don't have to borrow more than you need. This will also get you used to making debt payments before you start borrowing bigger amounts to expand your business.

- Microloans usually have very flexible repayment terms.

- Micro lenders will often play the role of advisors. Before giving you the loan, they will want to understand your business and might offer help with things such as drafting business plans and coming up with better sales and marketing plans.

- Micro lenders will often give you loans even if your credit score is not perfect.

Despite all these advantages, microloans also have some downsides, including:

- Micro lenders charge significantly higher interest rates compared to banks. Still, they are cheaper than other ways of raising funds, such as credit card loans.

- Microloans are, by definition, small loans. Therefore, if your business needs a lot of capital to get running, microloans might not work for you.

Chapter 24. Advantages of A Good Credit Score

You already know how bad credit can affect you and that it makes it even more important for you to establish a good credit score. It is going to make your financial life so much better and easy to deal with. There are so many benefits associated with having a good credit score and we are going to discuss them so that you can get motivated to maintain a good credit score yourself.

Better Chance of Loan Approval

When your credit score is in bad shape, you are always asked not to apply for any new loan or a credit card because it can affect your score even more negatively. Also, it is highly likely that you are going to be turned down yet again. It is also true that when your credit score is good, it does not automatically give you a guarantee that your loan is going to be approved. It definitely increases your chance at approval. There are so many other factors that the lenders have to check before finally agreeing to grant you the loan and a good credit score is just one factor. Your debt and your current income will also be taken into consideration. But when your credit score is good, you will have added confidence before applying for loans.

When your credit score is good, it reflects that you are a financially responsible person. So, when you go to the lenders or banks, they will not see you as a risk to them because your financial history shows that you pay back what you owe.

Get Low Interest Rates on Loans

When you borrow money, you have to pay it back at a certain rate of interest, and your credit score is what directly influences the rate of interest that you will be subjected to. When your credit score is good, lenders and banks are going to give you good interest rates and when you repay your loans or clear your credit card balances, then the financial charges that you are going to pay is quite low. The chances of you clearing off your debt faster will definitely be influenced by how much interest you have to pay. And when your credit score is good, you are paying a lesser amount of interest and this is saving you extra bucks that you can spend elsewhere.

Better Rates on Car Insurance

Getting car insurance is one of those things that is hugely impacted by your credit score. So, you should always try to maintain a good credit score if you plan to get car insurance. It is true that if your credit history is bad, then a company can be turning you down but on the other hand, if your credit score is good, you will get the chance to pay better and more affordable premiums. It is usually believed by these insurance companies that when a person has a bad credit score, they are more likely to file claims than others and this is the reason why they do not approve insurance to someone with bad credit history. But even if you manage to get the insurance, you will have to pay a lot more if you have bad credit when compared to someone with good credit.
Chances of Approval for Mortgage and Rental Applications Is Increased

Another sector that is highly influenced by better credit scores is when you are looking for a new home or apartment. A landlord and a tenant have a very similar relationship to that of a lender and borrower. And that is why a landlord always prefers to get involved with someone who is responsible for their financial life. Your landlord will want you to clear your rents within the due date just as the lender makes sure you are paying your monthly installments regularly.

It is because of this reason that many a time, you will find landlords asking for your credit score or your credit report before granting you access to the house and the same goes for rental companies. You will become a top-tier candidate the moment they find that your credit history is good and then, you will have to access more choices than the others.

Better Interest Rates on Mortgage

If you want to pay off your mortgage at a better rate of interest, then having a good credit score is definitely important. This is because there are thousands of dollars involved whenever you are trying to pay large loans like mortgages. Over such a long term, you are going to benefit a lot even if the rates of interest change by 1 or 2 percent. This will lead to a significant amount of savings which would have been otherwise wasted.

Moreover, lenders automatically find you attractive if you have a good credit score. Since mortgages run over an extended period of time, banks are always looking for people with good credit scores who will continue paying back during the entire term of the loan. This makes them see you as a lower risk candidate and offer you the best deals they have on mortgages.

Better Chance of Getting a Job

Yes, a good credit score can, in fact, impact your employment status as well. You will get jobs more easily when your credit history is good. This is because, in today's world, people are always looking for those candidates who will keep their promises and show good behavior. In short, they want the best people for their job. And many a time, these companies decide that by having a look at the credit history of that candidate. Before the company sends you an offer letter, they will ask your permission to have a look at your credit report, and sometimes, they will offer you a job only if you allow them to check your report. If your report states that there are a lot of late payments or bankruptcy records on your credit report, then they might simply give you a red flag and declare you not fit for the job they have.

Lower Security Deposits

Whether it is a long-term apartment or a simple vacation rental, a security deposit is often a mandatory thing. It becomes essential for you actually to get the rental. When you are asked to pay some amount of money upfront, then that is called a security deposit. It usually amounts to the rent of one to two months and the main purpose of a security deposit is to protect the rental company or the landlord from any kind of unforeseen expenses related to the occupancy or any damages. It is the security deposit that will be used if any kind of repair work has to be done after occupancy and whatever money is left will be paid back to the renter.

The amount of this security deposit is often lowered in amount if the renting company sees that you have a good credit score. Some people might not charge you any security deposit at all, but that is quite rare. On the contrary, your security deposits can become almost thousands of dollars if you have a poor credit report.

Better Chance of Approval for Credit Cards

This is exactly similar to what I said about a job or renting. Your credit cards will get approved easily if your credit score is in good health. It might not be the only factor to be considered for approval of credit cards, but it definitely is the most important one. If you do not have any credit scores at all or a very bad credit score, then you will automatically be categorized as a high-risk candidate which will instantly lower your chance of getting approved for a credit card. Similarly, when someone has a high credit score, they become favorable for the credit card companies and they get the best deals, and approvals become faster for them.

Get Higher Limits on Credit Cards

The benefits of having a good credit score do not stop at getting you a credit card but extend to other features as well. For example, you are going to get larger loans, higher limits on credit cards, and several such perks just because you have a good credit score.

When you have a good credit score, you might even be rewarded by your bank. In some cases, you are given access to more funds because the bank sees you as someone who repays what they owe on a regular basis. Some other perks that will come to you because of your good credit score are lower rates of interest, cashback programs, and rewards points.

These benefits are not only good for you but also for the bank. The interest that you accrue is what the banks profit from, whereas you profit from these amazing perks. When you are giving your payments on time, your credit score keeps improving.

Have More Negotiating Power

Whenever you are applying for a new loan or a credit card, having a good credit score means that you have the right and opportunity to negotiate with them so that you get a lower rate of interest. There are some other offers as well that you can access, and they will, in turn, depend on how well you are at bargaining. But whenever your credit score is bad, you are not likely to be in any position to negotiate the loan terms or ask for any other options or offers. You will simply have to settle with what you are getting.

Cell Phone Benefits

When your credit score is bad, you are not going to get a contract from the cell phone providers. You will have to go for the expensive options that have those pay-as-you-go plans. So, until and unless you have become established with your provider, you will end up paying a lot more on your contract. But when you have a good credit record, you will not have to pay any kind of security deposit. You will also get to buy the latest phones at a much-discounted price and all you have to do is sign a contract.

Availability of More Credit Card Options

There are so many rewards and signup bonuses associated with the best credit cards, but you will be able to access them only when your credit score is good. Also, with a good credit score, your chances of approval for these credit cards will become way higher. On the contrary, your chances of getting approved will tank down when your score is low.

When you possess the best credit cards in the market, you also get so many gifts, merchandise, better cashback offers, and also better travel offers. Another reason to opt for the better credit cards is that you will be able to steer clear of any of the predatory lending processes like pawn shop loans, title loans, and payday loans. These are the type of loans you should watch out for because they will keep you trapped in the toxic cycle of debt, and they even charge quite a high rate of interest.

Chapter 25. Simple Strategies to Fix Your Credit

Fixing your credit is possible, and not as difficult as you have been made to believe. No matter how bad your credit score seems, the ways to magically boost it are, in fact, very simple and practical. Contrary to common myths that a credit score may become so poor that it cannot be fixed, no credit score cannot be fixed. Whenever you find the need to fix one, apply the following strategies:

1. Hire an expert: The reason you can manage your company is that you are quite intelligent, and in some way, everyone is. But no matter how good you are, it is always nice to have opinions of an expert in technical cases like this. You have definitely learned lessons as your credit score drastically falls and you struggle to get it up. It isn't a bad idea to hear a couple of incisive words from a colossus. They would help with your budget, plans, financial decisions and so forth. Services like these are sometimes charged and are sometimes free, depending on the motive of the organization or individual you approach. You may hire a credit or financial counselor, an economist, or a bankruptcy attorney, among other specialists.

2. Work on your history: Since you have some history to start with and you are starting over, it is always a good idea to review your history. You should find out what you did wrong in each case, what was right and should have been enforced in your transactions. Terms that

would be convenient for your business. Policies you can conveniently subscribe to and those you shouldn't ever consider no matter how juicy they seem. You should be on the lookout for errors you didn't note as well, who charged exorbitantly, whom you can bank on for further business deals and so on.

3. Be updated on your credit score: It is a new season and you want to enjoy all the blessings it brings, shutting your eyes, hard as you can, on the other side. One of the ways you can do this is to start monitoring your credit report, so it doesn't ever go bad again. No matter how bad it seems already, you are bound to get the best out of it the moment you are always updated with your credit scores and your credit report in general. You have to think about the position of your credit and make informed decisions in your finances every time. Gradually, you can boost your credit scores this way. Besides, you need to keep your eyes on the credit report and your credit bureaus. You deserve a spick-and-span record this time and you shouldn't avoid lapses that can ruin that. So, be updated on your credit information and consider that every time you make financial decisions.

4. Do not close your old accounts: Whether your accounts have become delinquent or got to a point you don't want to associate with them, it is always recommended that you still keep them open in some way. Keeping accounts open can serve as an advantage in further credit transactions where they could prove your

experience with loans. If you must close an account, however, be sure there is no debt or balance to be covered in it as that can be a big minus to your new account. In fact, it is highly recommended that you avoid creating new credit records at this point.

5. Reach out to your creditors: Now this is interesting. A lot of people do not see the need to reach their creditors after their loans have been activated. Especially if they can afford the charges and there seems no reason to be in touch. But that's not right. It is not always the case that you can pay your monthly dues. Sometimes, you may have huge plans or investments that can't wait till the coming month and your best way to hit this is your monthly debt. If you are in touch with them, establishing firmly that you appreciate their business interaction and you do not mind relating with them beyond the current contract, you will be glad you did. You can count on them at such moments to be lenient and find some way to ensure your credit score is not affected. In fact, a lot of business transactions are conducted on the grounds of the good relationship between the key figures in the business.

6. Be patient: your credit score didn't deteriorate in hours; you should expect attempts to rebuild it to take some time too. The different steps you take will not yield many positive results immediately, certainly not as much as you'd like. But it's no reason to despair. It is certainly possible to build it again and it will happen if you are consistent. Do not mind how long the process

seems, it always works for those who are consistent. As Harry Hans of Financial times would say.

7. Avoid unnecessary credits: You surely remember that the federal court on Bankruptcy declared in 2013 that over 70% of unsecured debts are incurred on purchases that could be avoided. You don't want to add a penny to that percentage. It is why you should avoid purchasing items that do not appear in your budget. You should also limit the rate at which you explore markets and rake home some niceties, courtesy of your credit card. You can hit a nice score again, if you take those tips. None of these is a particularly new principle. They are all simple and practical. Ensure you keep them at heart.

Chapter 26. Dealing with Unforeseen Circumstances and Sudden Catastrophes

Though we may do our best always to be prepared, there are some unfortunate circumstances that can really shake up our lives, not to mention our financial situation. Abruptly losing a source of income because you are laid off or because of an injury or illness that prevents you from working can be devastating to our fiscal health, and doubly so if we do not take proper precautions ahead of time. The death of a loved one can also worsen your financial burden, as you may end up taking on some of their debts and managing their financial situation in the wake of their passing. This can all be complicated by the grieving process, which can make it more difficult to process the loss and maintain your income.

Job Loss

Job loss is one of the most common causes of financial hardship. It can mean losing your primary or supplemental income, and in some cases can mean losing your household's only source of income. The good news is that a loss of income does not automatically damage your credit score. The bad news is that, understandably, a job loss makes it hard to pay off debts, as you no longer have access to the money you were once using. Luckily, there are still some ways you can recover from a job loss and mitigate its effect on your debt repayment while you search for a new income.

1. Difficulty Making Payments

Getting fired or laid off can make it very difficult to stay on top of your debt payments. If you were previously paying a few hundred dollars in various bills each month, it is unlikely that the salary you get from unemployment or other sources between jobs will be enough to cover all of it. Unemployment generally pays much lower "wages" than what you earned while working, and even getting a new job can leave you rushing into a job with a lower salary just because you cannot afford to wait long enough to obtain a better one. All this can lead to a more restricted cash flow and a great deal of stress attempting to restructure your finances.

If you are having difficulty making your debt payments, you can use some of the methods we have mentioned for consolidating debts and limiting purchases to decrease your monthly debt burden. This will hopefully allow you to stay afloat in between jobs without impacting your credit score too severely. If you need additional help, you may have to take out loans or open up new credit accounts, both of which can damage your credit score. However, there are some alternative methods you can use to ensure you are still able to make at least the minimum necessary payments without hurting your credit irreparably.

2. Emergency Savings

Job loss is a perfect time to dip into your emergency savings, provided you had the forethought to save money. Unfortunately, many people do not think to have this cushion in place until they need it, and because of this they are unprepared when hardship strikes. If you are not already doing so, you should try to save a small portion of your paycheck each month as a rainy-day fund. It can save you a great deal of trouble further down the line and keep you from having to take out extensive loans to cover your bills. Of course, this is not something you can do once you lose your job, which is why it is imperative to start taking action early.

3. Eliminating Unnecessary Expenditures

When a job loss occurs, it may be time to reexamine what you are paying for and how necessary each item is. Consider what things you really use and which ones you simply keep around out of some vague sense that you might use them in the future. This is true for entertainment items especially. Look at things like cable TV and see if you can save by switching to alternatives and "cutting the cord." Alternatively, keep cable and eliminate streaming services you use rarely if at all. You can keep habitually paying for services like Netflix and Hulu simply because you have always paid for them, but if you are not currently watching anything, you can cancel payments for now and pick them back up should you need access to the service again in the future.

Aside from entertainment, be sure to limit your spending in stores. You can engage in coupon clipping or deal hunting at the grocery store. You can try to keep your clothing and shoe purchases to a minimum when you have a limited income as well, or shop at thrift stores for clothing and household goods. Only buy what you actually need and avoid anything that you might wear once or twice only for it to sit in the back of your closet for months. This same rule can apply to purchases from most types of stores. If you are not going to get your money's worth out of it, think twice about buying it when you are tight on funds.

4. Contact Creditors

Finally, if your job situation changes, get in contact with your creditors. You are certainly not the first person to have lost their job while paying back a loan or credit card debt. Your credit company may be able to offer you a lower monthly payment or another way to refinance your loan that ensures you can continue to make payments of some kind without putting your credit score at risk. The sooner you discuss this shift in your life with your creditors, the more amicable they will be to change your payment schedule, especially if you have gotten past payments in on time without issue.

Injury and Illness

In some cases, your source of income will be jeopardized as a result of sickness or an injury that leads to a temporary or permanent inability to work. For illnesses, you might develop a severe infection that only lasts for a week but makes it impossible for you to return to work during that time, or you might have a more serious medical condition that continues to impact your health for months or years. Injuries can be equally varied, with some only requiring rest and recovery for a few days and others needing a much longer period of time to mend if they mend at all. In these cases, you will find that maintaining your current income level and repaying your debts is more difficult.

5. Medical Expenses

On top of the interference with your ability to work, injuries and illnesses can introduce additional difficulties in the form of medical bills. Medical bills of any kind can be expensive, even for one-off hospital visits, but chronic conditions that require repeated doctor's visits can grow very expensive very quickly. If you don't have the best insurance, you can quickly find yourself swamped in debt from medical bills alone, not to mention your regular payments. Because of this, it is always a good idea to keep the aforementioned emergency fund. It may not be enough to pay a medical bill in full, but it can certainly help you make payments while you are unable to return to work.

If you cannot afford your bills, you can try to discuss a repayment plan with the doctor's office or hospital. You can also apply for financial assistance or work with a medical bill advocate to reduce any instances of overcharging on your account. Should you still have difficulty paying all your expenses, you may qualify for sick pay or a hardship withdrawal.

6. Alternative Incomes

If you will be out of your usual work for a long time, or if an injury has left you permanently unable to do your prior job, it may be time to look for a new source of income. Start looking for jobs that suit your unique conditions. If you have a busy schedule and need to be able to work at odd hours, look for night jobs or ones where you can work from home and set your own schedule. If you have difficulty with certain physical activity or standing for long periods of time, look for jobs that are primarily at a desk and let you sit for the duration of your shift. You might also consider starting your own business, which allows you to dictate your own hours and often work from home. Whatever your situation, there are jobs that will allow you to continue earning an income, even if they are not ideal for the long run - they can help you get through and maintain your credit.

Death In The Family

A death in the family is a very tragic event. You can feel that a lot of your time is taken up by grieving and learning to deal with the loss, and you may need to take time off work. Unfortunately, other aspects of your life — more specifically, your debts — are not put on hold because of a personal loss. Funeral arrangements can be costly affairs, and depending on your relationship with the deceased, you may become responsible for paying for some of their debts too. If you both contributed to the household income, you take on their half of your shared debts as well, which can be difficult on half the income you previously had. Still, there are some steps you can take to make this process easier on yourself and ensure it does not bankrupt you.

7. Requesting an Account Freeze

Credit bureaus are not aware that a death has occurred until it is reported to them. If you are the executor of your loved one's will, you should let the credit bureaus know that your loved one has passed away, as soon as possible. This allows them to put an account freeze in place, which prevents anyone from taking out accounts under their name. You only need to notify one of the three main credit bureaus, which will then notify the other two in turn. You should also notify the various creditors that managed your loved one's accounts so that the accounts can be closed.

8. Inheriting Debts

Occasionally, you will inherit debt after a death. After death, a person's estate is used to pay off their remaining debts before the remainder is left to those in their will; this is known as probate. Usually, probate is enough to cover most debts, as physical property and liquid assets can be used to make payments. Whatever debt may be left over is then dissolved most of the time, but there are some debts that are then transferred on to family members. For example, whoever inherits the house becomes responsible for the mortgage and home equity loan, and the inheritor of the car often ends up making auto loan payments. Most other inherited debts are conditional. Remaining credit card debt may simply disappear, but if you jointly owned them with your loved one, they can become your burden; the same is true of cosigned student loans.

Chapter 27. Personal or Business Credit Card?

A personal credit score will be between 300 and 850. A score in the high 700s will be an attractive customer for credit agencies. A high credit score can have many benefits. You can negotiate better deals, qualify for additional credit more easily, and be offered some of the best credit terms available. Business credit cards offer similar rewards to personal credit cards, but you will only get these if the business has a good credit score. Most of the rewards for business will be in the form of a cash back percentage on the purchases made with the business credit card. You are effectively saving money with every purchase. The business can often use the cash back to pay for reduced flight fares, which is highly beneficial if your employees need to travel for work.

Business credit card balances don't show on your personal credit unless you personally guarantee them or miss payments.

Therefore, any purchases made with a business credit card will not adversely affect your scores. Even if you max out your business credit card month after month, it will not hurt your personal credit score. Unfortunately, the balances you carry with your PERSONAL credit cards affects your scores more than almost anything else.

The Do's and Don'ts of Managing Your Credit

One of the most common things that I hear from people I meet, and help is: Tell me what to do. That is actually a very powerful statement: "Tell me what to do." For one, it means that people have started to take the first steps towards improving not only their credit, but their lives as well. It also means that people trust me to help them.

DO: Always, always pay on time. Considering that your payment history is the biggest percentage when it comes to calculating your credit score, it is crucial that you make all payments punctually. If possible, make credit card payments before the reporting date.

DON'T: Be late or miss a payment; once again, payment history is one of the biggest components used when calculating your FICO Score. Making late payments can lead to serious consequences. You can be charged a late fee, your interest rates may rise, the late payment marking will be reflected on your credit report, and your credit score may sink.

DO: Watch your usage of available credit. Remember that utilization plays a big role in your credit scoring. If you have credit cards that are maxed out, your credit score will suffer.

DON'T: Max out any of your credit cards. If you have a few credit cards but one of them is your absolute favorite, try to spread out the usage. If one credit card is maxed out, don't be afraid to transfer balances so that you can meet the 30% mark. Also make sure that the credit card or cards with the higher limits get paid off first.

DO: Age your accounts. Simply, the older your accounts, the better. Recall that Length of History was a component of your credit scoring. Aging your accounts will help to improve your credit file and credit score.

DON'T: Close older accounts. I have seen many people make the mistake of closing older accounts because they do not use them anymore. It is far from a good idea to do this. Also try to avoid opening too many new accounts; this brings the age average down.

DO: Make sure to minimize new credit. You don't want to open up too many new accounts too fast. Doing so would affect the aging of your accounts as mentioned.

DON'T: Make too many inquiries. An inquiry is simply whenever you, or someone else, requests your credit file. There are two types of inquiries: a hard pull and a soft pull. A soft pull inquiry does not have the same potential for credit disaster as a hard pull possesses. A hard pull occurs when you request your credit file to apply for credit (credit cards, car, house etc.) A soft pull occurs when companies request your file in order to make you credit card offers and such.

DO: Mix up your accounts and add variety. If you were to submit a résumé to an employer, the more work experience and variety you presented, the more likely you are to be hired. By adding variety to your file, you are showing that you know how to manage your credit in more than one way.

The Secret to Success

The value of credit is highly underestimated, and it is done so on purpose. If everyone knew the true value of credit and how to make it work for them, there would be an overflow of successful people and perhaps even more millionaires. The business of lending is one of the biggest industries on earth due to the trillions of dollars being exchanged at varying interest rates. The lower your credit score, the higher the interest rate; the higher the interest rates, the more you pay and the more they make. Saving 1% on an interest rate can be the difference in tens of thousands of dollars. It is clear to see that credit is important and valuable. But let's discuss how it can make you successful.

Making powerful investments in life, such as real estate or opening up a business can take tons of money and it can take more money than most people have available. This is where the value of credit comes in. With a good credit score, making investments without having the cash is extremely possible. When you build your credit file exactly the way it's supposed to be, it makes it so much easier for lenders to decide to loan you money no matter what type of purchase or investment you wish to make.

When it comes to opening a business, banks are willing to give small business startup loans to get a business off the ground, but it all depends on your credit score. They want someone who is guaranteed to repay the money, a Personal Guarantor. So, no matter what you are doing: making a big purchase, starting up a new business, or being a real estate mogul, your credit will always be a major decision factor. This is the reason why credit is the secret to success and taking care of your credit can truly lead to the American Dream or at least financial stability. Many of the world's richest people were not born with money but made their fortune through knowledge and innovation.

Chapter 28. Protecting Your Financial Privacy

Today, personal details about your life can be accessed with a mere push of a button. In fact, just about anything is available for sale, including your employment history, medical records, marital status and details about where you live. Several companies maintain thousands of different databases developed from a wide variety of public records, including birth and wedding announcements, telephone directories, voter registration records, motor vehicle records, and court filings.

Often times the information in one database is combined with information from another to create marketable new information products or to improve existing databases. In other situations, information from one database may be compared with that of another to help identify consumers with particular characteristics or to make an existing database more comprehensive and accurate. Databases are also being linked electronically to create huge information networks.

Personal information has become a valuable commodity. Yet the majority of the time we are unaware that the information about our finances, personal habits, health, buying patterns, and other such information is being bought, sold, and exchanged, nor are we aware as to where that information originates from. Even worse, there is little that can be done to stop what is happening with our personal information.

Unauthorized Access and Use of Credit Report Data
Unauthorized access to consumer credit files is easily obtained, especially now that online access is available from all major credit bureaus. Some businesses are misrepresenting themselves to gain access to credit bureau data. In some instances, those who have a legitimate reason to access credit record data are using that information for illegal purposes in violation of federal law or are selling it to others for unauthorized uses.

Although recent changes to the FCRA attempt to restrict who has access to credit record data, there is no reason to believe the problem will stop, considering the huge earnings potential that businesses and individuals can realize from consumer credit record data. Credit bureaus do not adequately police what their subscribers do with the consumer credit information in their files once they have it. Although laws are in place to minimize problems, the potential for fraud remains.

Federal Privacy Laws
Today, some of the most personal details of your life are being searched through and seized using technology rather than by physical means. As a result, most of the federal privacy laws that currently exist, including the FCRA, are inadequate. Not only are these laws outdated, but many are full of loopholes and exemptions that make them easy to bypass. In addition to the FCRA, the most significant federal privacy laws are the Privacy Act of 1974, the Right to Financial Privacy Act of 1978, the Video Privacy Protection Act, and the Computer Matching and Privacy Protection Act.

The Privacy Act of 1974
The privacy act of 1974 applies to federal agencies, prohibiting them from obtaining data for one purpose and then using it for another. The exception to the law applies when information is shared for "routine use," which essentially makes the law useless because any use can be interpreted as "routine".

The Right to Financial Privacy Act

Even though the Right to Financial Privacy Act is supposed to govern access of federal agencies to your bank records, exemptions allow U.S. attorneys and the FBI to review bank records. This law also does not apply to private employers or to local and state governments. Furthermore, new exceptions are added to this law annually, continuously limiting the power of the law to protect your financial privacy truly.

The Video Privacy Protection Act

The Video Privacy Protection Act prohibits retailers from providing a list of the videos you rent unless you approve the release of that information or a court order is issued ordering the release.

The Computer Matching and Privacy Protection Act

The Computer Matching and Privacy Protection Act regulates the federal governments use of computer matching techniques that compare information in one computer file to data in another to determine your eligibility for federal benefits. The law also limits the federal government's use of matching techniques to help it collect money, such as taxes. The law does not apply to all entities who may conduct potential matches, including matches done for law enforcement purposes.

Prescreening

Prescreening is a process by which a credit bureau creates a list of consumers qualified to receive a preapproved offer of credit using the information in its credit files. Prescreening can be done in one of two ways. First, a company may supply a credit bureau with a set of credit granting characteristics that describe its target market. For example, a credit card company may want to offer a preapproved card to all consumers who make over $100,000 a year and have flawless credit records and several lines of unused credit.

The credit bureau doing the prescreening will compare the criteria specified by the credit card company with characteristics of the consumers in its database. From this comparison, a list of prescreened consumers will be created for the credit card company to market its offer to.

A company may also provide a credit bureau with a list of criteria defining the types of consumers to whom it wants to market to, the credit bureau will then compare the information it has in its database with the criteria the creditor has specified in order to identify who should receive that company's offer.

The practice of prescreening if often criticized because it is done without the knowledge of consumers. Even though the company that purchases the prescreened list does not actually view the credit files of the consumers on the list, concern exists because technology has helped credit bureaus refine the criteria that can be used in the prescreening process. As a result, companies can now obtain specific details about your financial life without ever seeing your credit history.

Chapter 29. Your Financial Freedom

Financial freedom is a concept that people love to think about but rarely feel like they can reach.

What Is Meant by Financial Freedom?

Financial freedom has no set definition. However, it typically means that you are living comfortably and saving for retirement and in general. It can also mean that you have an emergency reserve set up. In general, financial freedom can mean whatever you want it to mean for you. For example, a prior college student may not think that financial freedom includes paying off all their student loans. This is because, at least in this day and age, a college student who needs to pay their own way realizes they will always be paying off their student loans. However, they might feel that student loans are the only debt they should have. Therefore, being able to pay off credit cards or medical bills leads them to financial freedom.

Some people might feel that financial freedom indicates they have absolutely no debt or loans. This includes them having paid off their mortgage and any car loans. They might also feel that in order to reach financial freedom, they need to be investing in a CD, bond, or even in the stock market.

Other people may feel that financial freedom means they are no longer tied down to a job. They are able to live off of their savings or a passive income, and they are able to retire and enjoy life through traveling.

Credit Cards and Financial Freedom - Is It Safe?

One of the biggest questions people have when it comes to financial freedom is whether they can have any credit card accounts in their name. While you may not owe anything on your credit cards (in fact, you might only owe one which you pay off in full every month), is this still financial freedom? In general, this is completely determined by your definition of financial freedom. However, if you ever find yourself not being able to pay off your credit card every month, this is not financial freedom. In most cases, financial freedom does mean you no longer have any debt, or at least that you are free from unnecessary debt, such as credit cards.

Most people are quick to state that financial freedom and credit cards do not go together simply because they are not safe with each other. This is due to the fact that it is often easy to fall back into thinking you can pay the amount off everything each month and then you become unable to do so. In general, people who reach financial freedom feel that credit cards allow for more of a trap and keep them from ever reaching financial freedom.

However, other people who feel they have reached financial freedom state that as long as you can manage your credit cards wisely, they can be included with your freedom. Some of them also advise that you set up a financial freedom plan. Within this plan, you will state your conditions of using a credit card. Of course, you need to be self-disciplined enough to follow your condition.

The Best Habits to Help You Reach and Protect Your Financial Freedom

When it comes to financial freedom, there are dozens of habits and tips that people provide in order to help you reach your financial freedom. It is important to note that because financial freedom can vary depending on the person's definition, some of the tips and habits might work for you while others may not. You need to find the ones that work best for you, not the ones that other people say are the best. Therefore, I am going to give you a fairly large list as I want you to make sure that you can find some of the best habits and tips so you can not only reach financial freedom but also protect it.

9. Make a Budget

Making and keeping a budget is one of the first steps everyone should take while heading towards your financial freedom. Even though you might find yourself changing your budget now and then, as you will add or delete bills or receive a different income, you always want to follow it. Not only will this help you in reaching your financial freedom but continuing to follow your budget will also protect your financial freedom.

Furthermore, creating a monthly budget can make sure that all your bills are being paid and you know exactly where your money is going. For example, you will be able to see how much money you spend on groceries, gas, and eating out at restaurants. This will help you know where you can decrease your spending, which will allow you to save more. There are a lot of great benefits when it comes to creating and sticking with a household budget.

10. Set Up Automatic Savings Account

If you work for an organization that will automatically place a certain percentage of your check into a savings account, take advantage of this. It gives you the idea that you never had the money to begin with, which means you don't plan for it and you won't find yourself taking the money out of savings unless you need it for an emergency. Furthermore, you can set up a separate savings account where this money will go. You can make it, so you rarely see this account, however, you want to make sure that your money is deposited, and everything looks right on your account. But, the point of this account if you do not touch it, even if you have an emergency. Instead, you will set up a different account for emergency basis.
The other idea to this is you pay yourself first. This is often something that people don't think about because they are more worried about paying off their debt. However, many financial advisors say that you are always number one when it comes to your finances. While you want to pay your bills, you also need to make sure that you and your family are taken care of.

11. Keep Your Credit in Mind Without Obsessing Over It

Your credit score is important, but it is not the most important thing in the world. People often fall into the trap of becoming obsessed over their credit score, especially when they are trying to improve it. One factor to remember is that your credit score is typically only updated every so often. Therefore, you can decide to set time aside every quarter to check on your credit report. When you do this, you not only want to check your score, but you also want to check what the credit bureaus are reporting. Just like you want to make sure everything is correct on your bank account; you want to do the same thing for your credit report.

12. It Is Fine to Live Below Your Means

One of the biggest factors of financial freedom and being able to maintain it is you can make your bills and comfortably live throughout the month. In order to do this, you need to make sure that the money coming into your home is more than the money going out. In other words, you want to live below your means.

This is often difficult for a lot of people because they want to have what other people have. They want to have the newer vehicles, the bigger boat, the newest grill, or anything else. People like to have what their friends and neighbors have. However, one-factor people don't think about is that their friends and neighbors probably don't have financial freedom. Therefore, you want to take a moment to think about what is more important for you. Would you rather be in debt like your friends or you would rather have financial freedom?

13. Speak with a Financial Advisor

Sometimes the best steps we can take when we are working towards financial freedom is to talk with a financial advisor. They can often give up information and help us with a budget, ways to make sure that we get the most out of our income, and also tell us where we might be spending more money than we should. Furthermore, they can help you figure out what the best investments are, which are always helpful when you are looking at financial freedom. At the same time, they can help you plan for your retirement, which is one of the biggest ways you will be able to remain financially free.

14. Completely Pay Off Your Credit Cards

If you are high-interest credit cards, which is often the case, you want to make sure that you pay these off every month. Therefore, your credit card spending should become part of your budget. What this means is you don't want to use your credit card for whatever you feel like. Instead, you want to create a list on when you can and when you can't use your credit card. For example, you might agree that it is fine in emergency situations or during Christmas shopping. You might also feel that you can use it during tips because it has trip insurance attached to it. Whatever you decide, you want to make sure you follow.

You also want to make sure that you pay off any high-interest loans. When it comes to loans that are lower in interest, they won't affect you too much.

15. Track Your Spending

Along with making sure you follow your budget; you also want to track your spending. There are several reasons for this. First, it will help you make sure that your budget is on track. We often forget about automatic bills that are paid monthly or don't realize how much we really spend every month. These factors can make our budget off, which can cause an obstacle when you are working to reaching and keeping your financial freedom.

Fortunately, there are a lot of apps that you can download, many of them are free, which will allow you to track your spending easily. Some of these apps include Mint or Personal Capital. These apps typically give you all the information you need and will automatically tell you how much you are spending and how much income you still hold at the end of the month. Most of these apps will also give you charts to help you see your spending habits in a different way.

16. Make Sure to Keep Your Mindset

This is a mindset that you will want to continue to have while you are living financially free. With this mindset, you will not only feel grateful for where you are in life, but you will also remember where you once were. This will help you work towards protecting your financial freedom instead of falling back into credit card debt.

Of course, you can adjust your mindset the way you want to once you reach financial freedom. However, you will want to make sure that you keep your mindset positive. After all, a positive mindset makes you believe that you can accomplish anything.

Chapter 30. How to Get Lender Offers?

A vast majority of lenders don't have offers that are clearly defined up front, instead they have a general loan package that can be tweaked based on the situation individuals who come to them find themselves in. With this in mind, it becomes apparent why it is so important to seek out multiple offers before making a decision.

Depending on your FICO score, lenders may be more than happy to compete for your business. This fact coupled with the lack of predetermined rates means that you can easily improve your results by shopping around and then singling out lenders who almost have the rates you are looking for and then telling them that you can get a better deal elsewhere.

To maximize this strategy, you are going to want to make a list of the features you are absolutely going to need to be happy with a given loan and then call each lender you have already talked to and go down the list point by point. If you come across a lender who has an approach that appeals to you, let the other lenders know about it and see what they can do to either match or beat it. They know they are in a competitive business and if you are willing to force their hand, they will show you just how much they want your business.

Pre-approved offers: If you took advantage of OptOutPrescreen.com to limit soft inquiries on your credit report and are planning on looking for lenders anytime soon then you may want to reconsider and opt back in, at least for the relatively near future. If you have not opted out of the system, and your credit isn't terrible, then putting in an application with one lender will likely trigger a barrage of competing offers from other lenders as creditors will happily provide your information to anyone and everyone who is interested in selling you on their services.

While this can be annoying in some cases, if you are looking for the best lender possible then it could be just what you need to pit several lenders against one another. Prescreened offers can make it easier for you to compare relative costs or special offers as long as you do your due diligence with each and ensure that you aren't being hornswoggled by smoke and mirrors.

Ensure you have a loan estimate document: The loan estimate document was created by the Consumer Financial Protection Bureau to make it easier for borrowers to compare the various costs associated with individual loans and lenders. Its job is to standardize and simplify the way that lenders expose their fees so that you aren't comparing apples to oranges. The loan estimate document can be downloaded from ConsumerFinance.gov.

In addition to make it easier to compare various potential loans, it makes it easy to be aware of the various fees that are sure to pile up along the way, even with the most apparently straightforward of loans. It also breaks down costs in a way that anyone can understand without the help of a CPA. It includes all sorts of useful information including estimated monthly payments, prepayment penalties and the interest rate of the various loans in question.

Lock in the best rate: Once you have done the work of comparing the various options available to you, the next thing you are going to want to do is to ensure that the best option doesn't change while you are making all of the relevant arrangements. To ensure this is the case you are going to want to ask the lender for a written rate lock or lock-in. This is a written and legally binding guarantee that the lender will give you the interest rate you discussed for the price you discussed for a set period of time. It protects you from interest rate increases that may occur while your loan is being processed. It is important to keep in mind that some lenders will charge for a lock-in while others will not it all depends on the individual lender.

Chapter 31. The Best Ways to Maximize Your Credit Score

The way to gain a good reputation is to endeavor to be what you desire to appear. Socrates

Alright, enough with all the background info! How to raise your credit score. Sure, if you follow the advice you've read so far, odds are you'll raise your score without even trying.

1. Get a Credit Card

Did you know that a person who doesn't use any credit cards at all is generally seen as a higher risk than someone who has shown that they use credit cards responsibly? Although surprising at first glance, its kind of makes sense if you think about it.

Part of your credit score is based on the types of credit accounts that you have. It is generally recommended that you try to get experience with different types of credit, and credit cards are one of the easiest forms of credit to obtain. And let's face it, despite the bad rap that credit cards get, they're actually pretty harmless if all you get is a card with a zero monthly fee and pay it off in full each month.

The guy or gal who has never had a credit card is kind of a total unknown — will they pay on time when given credit? Or will they blow it? Potential lenders have no way of knowing, and that makes them nervous.

So, don't be an unknown. Show the credit card companies and other lenders that you can be trusted with credit, and that you are able to keep up with your obligations.

2. Use Your Credit Card

See, you can do one better than just having a credit card. If you don't use your credit cards, they won't necessarily help your credit score as much as they should.

The ideal way to use your credit cards is to charge a small amount to them each month and pay it off in full when you receive your monthly statement. Use your credit cards for everyday purchases that you would have made anyways, such as groceries — this way, you won't be spending any extra money by using them.

Lenders need to know that you are good at making payments on time — and if you have no payments to make because you never actually use your credit card, then lenders won't have a clue. So, give them one, and reap the benefits of the good reputation you're building (and higher credit score that goes with it!) the next time you're negotiating a good rate on a mortgage or other loan.

But remember — the key is only to use a small percentage of available credit each month. Try to stick to using 30% or less of available credit.

3. Ask Your Credit Card Company to Raise Your Credit Limit

I know that asking your credit card company to raise your credit limit flies in the face of what many self-respecting credit users would do, right? Maybe you worry that if you ask for this, they'll think you're about to go on a massively irresponsible shopping spree and max out your card, right? But the thing is, raising your credit limit while keeping your spending levels the same can actually raise your credit score. This is because part of your credit score is based on the percentage of available credit that you use.

Assuming you have a good reputation with your credit card company and tend to pay on time, the odds are good that they'll be happy to accommodate your request for a higher limit. And besides, the worst that can happen is that they say no — aside from wounding your pride, nothing bad will happen.

I used to worry that when I did this, the credit card company would want to know why I wanted the higher limit. But to my surprise, they often don't even ask. And when they do, my response is usually one of the following:

"I have a large purchase coming up that I'd like to charge to my credit card for the reward points I'll get," or, "I'd just like to have the option of charging larger purchases to my card if I need to — it's cheaper than paying a fee to use my debit card." And I'm sure you can come up with many more reasons why a larger limit on your card would benefit you.

4. Apply for Another Credit Card

Ok, so in the short term, this can lower your credit score due to the credit check that will be run on you during the application process. But, if you're new card has a high enough credit limit, in the long run, your credit score could go up. You can maximize your chances of a long-term rise in your credit score if you keep your monthly spending the same. This way, the percentage of available credit that you are using will decrease — and that is the secret sauce to raising your score via this method. This strategy is best if:

1. *You can afford to take a small hit to your credit score in the short-term (i.e., your score will decrease at first, due to the credit check that will be run on you).*
2. *You will not increase your spending just because you have access to more credit.*

Caution

If you implement this strategy, I recommend that you go slow — add one new account at a time and monitor the effects that it has on your credit score.

Assuming all goes according to plan and your score rises in a few months, feel free to apply for another credit card. Wait and see what the effect is on your credit score this time (I recommend you wait a good six months to be sure of the effects), and if it rises, feel free to add another credit card to your collection.

Many experts recommend limiting your total number of credit cards to no more than three to five. But the thing is, there is no 100% hard and fast rule about this — everyone's credit file is different, and the algorithms that the credit bureaus use to calculate your score are very complex, thus making it hard to predict with certainty how many cards are too many for any one individual.

By adding one card at a time, and waiting several months in between adding a new account, you ensure that you minimize any risks by monitoring the results of any changes you make and being able to backtrack if needed.

I do not recommend that you add new accounts if you are planning on applying for important credit in the near future, such as a mortgage.

The Key to Success with This Strategy

Here are the keys to maximizing your odds of success with this strategy:

- Charge a small amount to the new credit card and pay it off in full each month.

- Ensure that your total spending across all credit accounts does not increase. (For example, if, before obtaining the new card, you charged $1000 in total per month to all of your credit cards combined, continue to charge no more than $1000 per month in total to all of your credit cards combined.)

- Pay off the balance on all of your credit cards in full, and on time, when you get your monthly statements.

3. Pay Off Your Credit Cards in Full Each Month

Being close to maxing out your credit cards is worse than using a small amount of your available credit. You see, people who are close to maxing out their credit cards are associated with a higher risk of defaulting or not being able to make future payments.

On the other hand, if you not only limit yourself to using a small amount of your available credit each month, and you pay off your credit cards in full, you'll be lumped in with the lower risk people and end up with a higher credit score than you would if you left that balance to grow with time.

The thing is, if you don't pay off your credit cards in full each month, odds are, the percentage of available credit that you are using will creep up every month. And as you can imagine, that percentage creep is likely to lower your credit score.

For example, Matt charges $500 each month to his credit card. He only makes the minimum payments, and within less than a year he ends up owing a few thousand dollars. This is his only credit card, and the limit is $5000. Within 10 months, he's easily maxed out his card, and that leads to a fall in his credit score. So, don't be like Matt. Pay off your credit card in full each month and enjoy the higher credit score that should result.

4. Keep Credit Balances to Less Than 30% of the Maximum Available Credit

Experts recommend keeping your credit balances to less than 30% of your maximum limit. Your credit score can take a moderate hit if the balance goes over 50%, and major hit if the balance goes over 75%.

5. Experience with Both Revolving and Installment Accounts Is Good

Part of your credit score is based on the types of credit accounts that you have experience with. By having experience with multiple kinds of credit, you can raise your score more than you would if you lacked variety on your credit report. You can start things off by getting some experience with credit cards, a type of revolving account.

Lines of Credit

A line of credit from your local bank is another kind of revolving account. I love lines of credit for the simple fact that having one on my checking account means I never have to worry about overdrawing my account with day-to-day purchases. And if its responsible use adds some variety to my credit report, all the better.

As long as you have the willpower not to max out your line of credit just because it's there, you ought to consider getting one if you haven't already.

Secured Installment Loans

Secured installment accounts include things like a car loan — whatever you are borrowing the money for is used as collateral for the loan (i.e., if you default on your loan, the lender gets the item you borrowed the money for in the first place). In addition to that, you'll have a fixed amount that you need to pay off each and every month, and the balance owing on the loan will decrease in time, until it reaches zero.

Secured installment loans can be a great way to increase your credit score because showing your ability to make a fixed monthly payment is an indicator of your reliability and financial stability.

This is very different from a credit card, where a person can vary the amount of their payments each month, depending on their cash flow.

Due to the interest charges you'll incur, I don't recommend that most people go out and get an installment loan just for the sake of helping their credit score. But, if you ever do require such a loan, it's nice to know that it might help your credit score in the long run.

Chapter 32. Managing Foreclosure/ Bankruptcy/Tax Lien and Other Judgments.

First, what are the public records you can expect on your credit profile?
According to Experian reports. Three kinds of horrible public records used to be displayed on a credit record. But not anymore. You may have heard and wild guesses about this, but straight from the horse's mouth, only one kind of public record is displayed in a credit report: Bankruptcy.
Don't ask me questions yet. I will tell you what Bankruptcy is about. But right before that, you need to know that Bankruptcy may be the only record that is displayed on your profile, but it certainly isn't the only thing you have got on your hands. Foreclosure is equally crucial. We will start with that, and then we will see how to handle the records on your profile. Here we go;

What is Foreclosure?

Foreclosure is used to describe an official situation where a lender takes control of the asset which debtor's stands in as collateral while applying for a loan. This means foreclosure occurs when a debtor uses some of his properties to stand as collateral, meaning that they can be sold if he doesn't pay up that money.
So, foreclosure is what happens when he doesn't pay that money. If you remember correctly, we referenced this while talking about some of the different types of loans you can have. Can you remember which? I am not telling you; you should have known.

Though foreclosure does nothing on your credit profile, it is strongly recommended that you should dodge it at all costs. Whatever you used as collateral must be something of considerable value to you. Probably your house (mortgage), your parcels of land, or some noteworthy machines. It hurts to see those things go.

Foreclosure is a long and arduous process too. It may span up to 700 days. So, even lenders try to avoid it if they can. Foreclosure usually takes place in different formats. Some are called Judicial, others Non-Judicial Foreclosure. The fundamental difference is that judicial foreclosure requires the lender to obtain official consent from the court before auctioning the property or seizing it. In Non-Judicial cases, the lender is not required to obtain court permissions. She could simply go on to seize the assets.

Just like every other loan, the easiest way to avoid foreclosure is to pay your loans promptly. Sometimes, I recommend you take loans to clear off your debts.

Now, Bankruptcy?

Bankruptcy is a financial declaration that a person is no longer capable of paying the debts he has acquired. It is a court proven declaration that a debtor has exhausted all means of getting the funds he owed and failed. And now, all creditors will have to be lenient with him. In some way, it sounds like a method of getting relief from your debts, if not all, some.

The introduction of Bankruptcy stemmed from the idea that a debtor cannot be killed for the loans she owed. It is also not the slavery age. As such, she can't be forced into slavery; neither can her children be swapped for her loans. What to do? Either let off of her or ease her paying methods.

It hasn't some rumps that you should understand if you are starting to think it is your way out already. You are required to declare all of your assets when you declare bankruptcy. For example, if you declare bankruptcy while having an outstanding of $80,000. You will state all of your personal resources, chairs, dresses, house, et cetera. It is then the job of the creditor to decide whether anyone holds value to him, and can be sold, seized or not. As it turns out, many people often lose more than they were hoping to when they declare bankruptcy, and it might turn a win-win situation for creditors.

Debtors realize this fact. And going by the records, we understand that many had given false statements or declarations, concealed assets, destroyed traceable documents, and so on. These acts are considered Bankruptcy Fraud and are heavily frowned upon by the US. If you are declaring bankruptcy, be set to face the full complications.

Bankruptcy is filed in a situation where a debtor declares that she is entirely incapable of paying further loans. She has tried all other methods, and she is left with no choice than to seek leniency from the court.

When this is approved, the debtor declares her total assets and they are liquidated, in other words, sold to cover whatever it could of the loans. Afterward, the debtor is completely absolved of further payments. The only problem is that it reflects on your credit score for ten consecutive years. This means that every potential creditor can understand that you have been in a financial mess at some point, and you had to give things which do not measure up to the value of the loan. That is never a good sign, and singularly, it will be the reason you will be turned many times all over the 20 years.

Bankruptcy is declared in a situation where a debtor is confident that he could pay the debts. But considering his current financial situation, he would be a long period to pay. This time could span into several years. In the end, a repayment plan is approved by the court, and the debtor pays over that period. He is absolved of the debt after payments. Bankruptcy reflects on your credit report for seven years. It faces a lot of criticism, and it could be a reason you're turned down too, but less likely

So, what can you do to maintain?

Prevention has always been better than cure. But if you are here already, it doesn't help to keep musing over the error you've made. Pick yourself up and be set to make a better impression in future endeavors. Try to pay other debts promptly. The more you perform better in other debts, the higher your chances of weakening the effects of bankruptcy on your profile.

Conclusion

When you invest money to take control of your financial freedom we always choose the option that gives us the greatest economic security possible, now we make much clearer what are the economic risks that can happen and how insurers can provide compensation not only emotional, but also economic, covering some financial loss for an unforeseen future, but many of the risks not supported by an insurer are those taken at the time when we venture to regain administrative control of our income and what we implement so that these grow as time goes by. However, these risks still have the probability of causing us to lose some or all of our investment, but if we don't, we move further and further away from the hope of meeting the goals we set for ourselves.
With a strong business credit profile built, a business can qualify for massive amounts of credit and funding. A business can secure store credit cards, Visa cards, MasterCard credit cards, even American Express cards.
A strong business credit profile also helps a business qualify for credit lines, loans, merchant advances, factoring, and many other sources of funding. Having access to large amounts of working capital is essential with helping the business grow into a healthy, profitable company.
Established business credit also adds value to the business. Any potential future sale of the business will greatly be benefited when the business has an already established positive business credit profile.
The stronger the profile, and more depth in trade lines, the more valuable the business becomes to investors and other parties who might be interested in purchasing the business in the future.

The business owner already has an established personal credit profile that can be leveraged for the business owner to be approved for credit and loans. With business credit established the business will have double the borrowing power as it will have access to the business credit, and the personal credit of the business owner.

Business credit can be used to obtain funding with no personal guarantee from the business owner, providing a major additional benefit when the business credit is being used instead of the business owner's personal credit.

A good business credit profile and score can be built much faster than a business owner can build their personal credit profile. And, business credit approvals tend to be higher dollar amounts than business owners see through personal credit approvals.

Credit limits on business credit accounts tend to be higher. It is easier and faster to get approved with multiple credit sources.

And it is easier to get approved for multiple credit cards or credit lines with individual business credit sources than it is with consumer credit approvals.

These are only some of the significant number of benefits that building business credit provides to a business and the business owner. For all these reasons, it is tough for any business to truly be successful without establishing a good business credit profile and score and leveraging that to help the business prosper.

You are now empowered with the knowledge and tools you need to ensure your business can obtain and maintain an excellent business credit profile and score. Put your knowledge to use today and get started on building business credit for your business or using business credit to help you start a new business venture.

Once you have built a positive business credit profile, you can finally have the positive business credit and financial future you deserve.

www.ingramcontent.com/pod-product-compliance
Lightning Source LLC
Chambersburg PA
CBHW071402210526
45465CB00001B/210